Women in Mexico: A Past Unveiled

Translations from Latin America Series

Women in Mexico:
A Past Unveiled

꘎꘎

By
Julia Tuñón Pablos

Translated by
Alan Hynds

University of Texas Press, Austin
Institute of Latin American Studies

Gage quotes were unavailable in the original English. Translations here
provided by Alan Hynds.

Originally published in 1987 as *Mujeres en México: Una historia olvidada.*
Copyright © 1987, Fascículos Planeta, Mexico City.

Fourth University of Texas Press printing, 2009

Requests for permission to reproduce material from this work should be
sent to Permissions, University of Texas Press, P.O. Box 7819, Austin, TX
78713-7819.

www.utexas.edu/utpress/about/bpermission.html

⊗ The paper used in this book meets the minimum requirements of
ANSI/NISO Z39.48-1992 (R1997) (Permanence of Paper).

Library of Congress Cataloging-in-Publication Data

Tuñón, Julia.
    [Mujeres en México. English]
    Women in Mexico : a past unveiled / by Julia Tuñón Pablos : translated
by Alan Hynds. — 1st ed.
        p. cm. — (Translations from Latin America series)
    Includes bibliographical references (p.) and index.

ISBN 978-0-292-78161-0 (pbk. : alk. paper)

    1. Women—Mexico—History.   I. Title.   II. Series.
    HQ1462.T8613   1999
    305.4'0972—dc21   98-51647

For Arnau

Contents

Photo section follows p. 62

Preface

жж

Since 1982 I have been seeking women in Mexico's past. As with any historical work, this one requires a strong vocation for searching and a high tolerance for disappointment—qualities that both fail me at times. Nevertheless, I find that to conduct research is a great privilege—at times a somewhat exhausting privilege, but a privilege nonetheless: that of plunging into an inquiry that is to a large extent an inquiry into myself as a member of a social group.

When six colleagues and I initiated the Seminar on Women at the National Institute of Anthropology and History (INAH), our common interest was—perhaps more than a precise understanding of women's historic issues—the concern we shared as women academics in social science fields at a specific time and in a specific place. My need to understand myself as a person was continually distorted by an occupational hazard: being a historian leads one to question oneself untiringly, to delve into processes, antecedents, interrelations—even when listening to the radio, watching a movie, speaking with an old man—and to do so conscious of being a woman, seeing the differences from and similarities with our mothers or daughters, and aware that one is part of a system. The seminar allowed me to study women—with all the pertinent academic justifications—as a historical subject that is recorded in the national process; but it also secretly gave me, personally, the prerogative to understand more clearly: perhaps not to understand more, but rather less, and from there to clarify what I don't know, what I need, what I seek, and what I attempt to do. Hence, the seminar allowed me to give a historical dimension to a life reality that I share with a group encompassing as much as half of the population. On a practical level, it provided all of us with the possibility to discuss—to discuss the effectiveness of a particular theoretical position, the quality or lack thereof in the material we had read, the criteria for putting together a bibliography—and, in sum, to ask ourselves: why, where, how, when, and for how long?

In 1985, I took advantage of a sabbatical year to spend three months in Spain and participate in the Seminar on Women's Studies at the Universidad Autónoma de Madrid. Once again, because of the same professional hazard mentioned above, I was besieged by questions: In what way am I, as a Mexican woman, like Spanish women? How and in what respects do our histories resemble each other? I was asked to write an essay on the participation of women in Mexico's development. Although the article, which I titled "A ojo de pájaro: La mujer mexicana en el proceso de integración nacional" (A bird's-eye view: Mexican women in the process of national integration), has never been published, writing it forced me to make an effort that I might not have made in Mexico, because of my propensity to paraphrase more than summarize. That article was a small, preliminary version of this book, first published in Spanish in 1987 by Editorial Planeta under the title *Mujeres en México: Una historia olvidada*. This book has been generous to me. Not only was the process of writing it intense and stimulating, but its reception by readers of both sexes made me feel that it had been worth the effort.

Because of this book, in 1992 my colleagues at the Interdisciplinary Program in Women's Studies (PIEM) at the Colegio de México invited me to teach a class on the history of women in Mexico, as part of the Specialization Course in Woman's Studies. The contact with other academics and with the students I taught from four different academic years—all women—was highly rewarding, since it forced me to remain focused on Mexican women's past, to update my bibliography, and to take care of sundry other tasks related to teaching.

The book has continued to give me surprises: The University of Texas at Austin—so prestigious in Mexican history topics—proposed that I republish it. With this stimulus, I set out to update my information, using the contributions of some excellent research projects conducted by my colleagues. In a single decade, research on Mexican women has been enriched significantly—so much so that I have begun to doubt the extent to which the history of Mexican women continues to be forgotten. In the ten years since the book was first published, I have added information, increasing the length of the book by 50 percent, and I have made the necessary theoretical revisions. Nevertheless, my intention for the book continues to be, as it was with the original edition, that it serve as a guide, provide information on the circumstances that have shaped Mexican women, awaken interests, and lead to inquiries.

In 1987 I thanked Marisol Arbeláez, Paola Costa, Concepción Ruiz Funes, Martha Rocha, Marcela Tostado, and Enriqueta Tuñón, colleagues of mine in the INAH Seminar on Women, for the work they had carried out with me. I also thanked my colleagues in Madrid: Pilar Folguera and María Ángeles Durán. And I thanked Carmen Ramos and

Carlos San Juan for their encouragement, Magalí Muriá and Esperanza Pablos for their help, and Francisco Borreguero and Ángeles Pablos for their kind hospitality in Madrid.

To this original list of names I would now like to add a few others: Julianne Burton, whose interest in Mexico brought her to read the text and who proposed that it be translated into English; Elena Urrutia, Luz Elena Gutiérrez de Velasco, Mercedes Barquet, Soledad González, Irma Saucedo, Dalia Barrera—teachers at the PIEM with whom I had the pleasure of vying for a space in which to work; Maru Peña, Elvia de la Vara, Esperanza Rojas, Carmen García, and Concepción Toledo, for their constant support in administrative matters; and Verónica Devers, for helping me with the typing.

I would also like to thank Alan Hynds, who did a very careful and professional job on the translation text, and Virginia Hagerty and Carolyn Palaima at the Institute of Latin American Studies, who helped make the publication of this translation possible.

Over the last ten years many other persons have guided and supported me; they are, however, so numerous, and their help has come in so many forms, that I prefer to express my gratitude to them personally and in the intimacy of a conversation.

As you can see, the gestation of this book has a long history, a history in which the project re-created its writer, thanks to the comments of students and colleagues and to the contributions made by new books and documents that have come my way and in which I have searched for new questions based on renewed concerns. I need only reiterate that this has been a generous book.

Introduction
Women in Mexico:
Between the Mirror and the Mirage

›◊‹◊

To ask ourselves questions about the role of women in Mexico's history implies that we are aware of many gaps in our knowledge. We know that women have been present, that they are a historical subject, and that their absence from historical sources does not imply their absence from the process through which the country has been built. The problem is how to fill these gaps. Inevitably, we will recall Virginia Woolf's description of her search for English women writers on the library shelves: "Women have served all these centuries as looking-glasses possessing the magic and delicious power of reflecting the figure of man at twice its natural size. . . . [given that] mirrors are essential to all violent and heroic action" (1957, 35–36).

Here Woolf suggests a possible answer to some of the questions asked today by those of us who look for women in history: the role of women has been distorted by the looking-glass, that is, by historiography. Their image has been distorted like a figure in a carnival mirror, making their struggles, their realities, and their life conceptions appear similar to those of the people who hold power, and it has inspired the traditional books about the muse of history, Clio. Women have been removed from the past, and only those who serve as the backdrop for a male personality (as mothers, wives, or lovers) have been exalted; on other occasions, they have been made into figures who imitate heroes, kings, or soldiers—extras in a historiography that has focused on politics, war, and prominent public events. In this manner, women—understood as a specific social group—have been closed off from the recognition that would be given them by a looking-glass that reflected a true image of themselves, that gave them a sustaining memory of common action and a possible project for the future.

The historical model of women that has been offered is a mirage telling us what they "should be." It alienates women from their realities and options. The concept of the feminine has been associated with "nature"; hence, the virtues characteristic of their gender border on the zoological: emotion, instinct, intuition. The "natural" appears as if it were eternal; by contrast, social things, things that are eminently human, are subject to change: through thought, through the making of culture, through creating. Thus, history has been considered intrinsically male. Women, like nature, are admired yet feared, sublimated yet despised. Human spheres have been dichotomized and stereotypes have been imposed: the ideal is for men and women to cease to be potentially complete persons and to limit their activities to the capacities that have been assigned to their genders; this dichotomization has crippled both genders. Women are not merely biology, just as men are not solely reason. Historiography needs to explode this myth, archetype, stereotype, mirage that robs both men and women of their possibilities—and that robs women of their humanness, of the possibility to change and grow. As a collective subject, women need a mirror that will return to them the possibility of being and acting. Historiography can attempt to give them a memory. This is the reason for making the effort.

How can we recover this historical subject within a social science discipline? How can we implement an approach that will allow us to recognize the specific actions that women carry out in the spheres that society has assigned to them? In what ways have new fields of action been opened up? Despite the research conducted on the topic, we have more questions than answers: questions that allude to the courses of action in and of themselves; to a particular chronology; to the interaction between class and gender, based on ethnic group, geographic area, the generation of the woman or women being studied; and questions that take into account women's relations with the male gender, with the men—also historical—who share a world with them.

This task entails myriad difficulties. To attempt to recover women from the archival wealth of the past is to assume from the start that women's existence was somehow recorded therein. But female actors have not always been included in archives. The information we do find has usually been filtered through criteria irrelevant to women's specificity.

Women's membership in the society to which they belong and their necessary assignment to one of the classes that make it up do not exclude them from being members of their society on the basis of their own gender situation, which both hinders and enriches studies on them. Consequently, we must return to the past and look at it in a different light, and we must diversify our sources: we must examine novels, folk songs and ballads, diaries, various types of statistics, travel memoirs, collections of letters, visual representations, and historiography based on oral history. We must do so in a manner that allows us to recover that which is specific to women: their unique power and weakness, outside the sphere of traditional politics; the relationship between their real lives and the control exercised through laws; their vision of the world, in terms of both their mentality and their senses; their labor, in both production and reproduction, as well as in the double workday. This also entails specifying the situations that cause their oppression, exploitation, or marginalization, when such conditions exist. In sum, we must resort to any and all criteria that will explain women's particular development as members of Mexican society.

I am aware that women as an absolute category exist only in the myth that attempts to construct an ahistorical "eternal woman." Even myths, however, portray a time, a concern, and a set of values and thus become testimonials for the social sciences. Throughout Mexico's history, women appear as the object of a twofold game: on the one hand, they are sublimated in myth; on the other, they participate in society as subjects subordinated by their biology.

A glance at the bibliography on women in Mexico points to the overwhelming significance of three historical figures: Malinche, the Virgin of Guadalupe, and Sor Juana Inés de la Cruz. All three have been made, each in her own manner, into gender archetypes because of the unique manner in which they took part in the nation's evolution. In them were deposited—absolutely and exclusively—traits that are normally commingled and confused and often contradict each other, so that these three archetypes became symbols disproportionate to their actual deeds: Malinche appears to monopolize sexuality; Sor Juana, the intellect; and Guadalupe, unselfish motherhood. The construction of these models makes the three personages a standard against which everyday women are compared: one can be as treacherous as Malinche, as sublime as the "Tenth Muse," or can more or less approach the *summum bonum*, Guadalupe: How unselfish and long-suffering were the *soldaderas* (women soldiers), and how important was their presence in the Revolution? To what degree do real mothers reproduce these values? Other figures, inhabitants more of the earth than of myth, such as Josefa Ortiz de Domínguez or La "Güera" Rodríguez, occupy a second plane, and activists such as Juana Belén Gutiérrez de Mendoza have a role that is clearly negligible when not altogether disregarded. Perhaps this tendency—which is, moreover, shared by other societies—can be observed all the way back to the pre-Hispanic world, as far back as the imbalance represented in the social position of women vis-à-vis the goddesses who occupied the religious pantheon. Indeed, even though indigenous beliefs expressed a clearly patriarchal system, female deities possessed an obvious personality—the natural reflection of an agrarian society. Later on, during the shaping of the Mexican nation, new elements further complicated their position.

The purpose of this book is to propose a series of directions that—perhaps—will help locate the role of women in Mexico's history; open up research options; disseminate concerns. In sum, this book hopes to contribute a grain of sand to the painstaking but fascinating project of constructing a historical memory of women for Mexico.

1

Women in the Mexica World
The Dilemma:
Eternal Goddesses or Mortal Women?

⋊⋉

The world prior to the 1521 Spanish Conquest was extremely complex. In the territory encompassed by present-day Mexico, myriad civilizations had arisen in two broad cultural spaces: Mesoamerica and Aridamerica.[1] The first, especially, was a land of splendor, since agriculture allowed for a sedentary life and a social organization that fomented the arts and sciences.

The southern boundary of Mesoamerica was located in Central America and ran from the Motagua River (on the Atlantic Coast of present-day Nicaragua) to the Nicoya Gulf (on the Pacific Coast of present-day Costa Rica). In the north, the boundary shifted depending on migration, which, in turn, was influenced by the weather; in the early sixteenth century, however, it consisted of a broad swath of land running roughly from the Lerma River in the west to the Pánuco River on the Gulf of Mexico. We have indications that Mesoamerica was inhabited as far back as 22,000 B.C.

Anthropologists and archeologists have used cultural traits to delineate periods or draw boundaries between them. Notwithstanding their linguistic and cultural differences, the various civilizations that flourished throughout Mesoamerica shared common traits, including polytheism, the use of a tool known as the *coa* (hoe) or *bastón plantador* (planting stick) for growing maize, and the practice of terracing land. Their political organization was based on theocracy. In architecture, they built graded pyramids. In science, they possessed a thorough knowledge of the stars, and they devised highly precise calendars. The leading cultures in the south were the Olmec (Tabasco and Veracruz), the Maya (Chiapas and the Yucatán Peninsula), the Zapotec and Mixtec (Oaxaca); in the central plateau, or altiplano, the Teotihuacán, Toltec, and Mexica were predominant.

In Aridamerica emerged cultures called Chichimec by their neighbors. Nomadic, highly warlike groups, the *chichimecas* made frequent incursions into the lands to the south in search of more favorable living conditions. One of these incursions was carried out by the Aztecs, who

founded the city of México Tenochtitlán in 1325 and who were henceforth called Mexicas.

When the Spaniards arrived on the Gulf coast in 1517 and advanced
inland in 1519, the Mexicas were the dominant culture in the complex
Mesoamerican mosaic; hence, it was mainly this group that fought
against the Spaniards.

For an understanding of the women who lived in this world, we must
rely almost exclusively on Roman Catholic sources. These data are
somewhat more vivid than those made available by other cultures in
Mexico, since they go beyond mere archeology and myth. Nevertheless,
it is evident that this information was filtered by the Spaniards with a
clear catechization purpose. Moreover, since the *cronistas* (chroniclers)
were pursuing a political project, their narrative focuses for the most part
on the conquest. Indigenous cultures were portrayed as a backdrop for
the actions of the conquerors. In recent years, our understanding of the
codices has improved greatly, and epigraphy is now enabling us to read
the stelae, a development that will surely lead to a better understanding
of the female sectors in these societies.

Mexica culture was profoundly religious. The gods governed humans'
lives, and some demanded periodic sacrifices in exchange for the continued protection of the species. The Mexicas' vast pantheon included the
deities of the peoples whom they had assimilated as their empire
expanded. Nevertheless, the theology of the educated elite included an
original principle that consisted of an androgynous deity, Ometeotl, the
Lord of Duality, who had both a male facet (Ometecuhtli) and a female
one (Omecihuatl), each of which was equally necessary. Gender division
was the axis around which all of society revolved; indeed, the natural
world was thought to be divided into male and female, which were
considered opposing, but complementary, principles (López Austin
1982, 145–147).[2] This duality is represented in many religious symbols
through which the feminine principle is given a specific importance. For
example, the sister or wife of the rain god, Tlaloc, is Chalchiuhtlicue,
who is the goddess of rivers and lakes and who drowns persons who swim
within her domains. The rulers of the netherworld were also two:
Mictlantecuhtli and Mictecihuatl. This organization into pairs gave
balance to the cosmos by distributing the functions needed for universal
harmony (López Austin 1982, 146). Nevertheless, the hierarchical status
held by women in the indigenous pantheon bore little resemblance to
that held by flesh-and-blood women in society.

Humans had been created from corn dough and given life through
divine sacrifice. They were therefore obligated to provide the gods with
sustenance through similar acts, offering them their most valued possession: human life.

The principal deities were male, although one female figure was central to the pantheon: the goddess Coatlicue, or Mother Earth, who, in her lunar persona of Tlazolteotl, was a goddess of eroticism and represented flesh, desire, and filth; she ate the foul matter produced by men and women and encouraged lasciviousness. In another version, she was also Chicomecoatl, the goddess of sustenance.

Coatlicue is a complex figure. The sculpture of her in Mexico City's Museum of Anthropology has been said to summarize Mexica thought and religiosity (Fernández 1959): her "feet" are claws; she wears a skirt of intertwined serpents, a necklace with alternating hands and hearts, and a belt clasped with a skull. On her back she carries plumed headdresses. At the ends of her arms she has snake heads, and from her neck arise, in lieu of a head, two hideous serpents. According to myth, Coatlicue is the mother of Huitzilopochtli, the sun god of war, who had been conceived by a feather that came loose from Coatlicue's broom while she was cleaning a temple. Her pregnancy scandalized her daughter, Coyolxauqui (the moon), who convinced her four hundred brothers (the stars) to kill their mother. Just as they were about to attack, Huitzilopochtli was born, ready to defend Coatlicue and armed with his *xiuhcoatl*, or "fire serpent," opposing the darkness with light. This tradition has been interpreted as women's loss of power to men.

Huitzilopochtli, in his role as Ollintonatiuh (Sun in Motion), must struggle each night against Tezcatlipoca, the god of the underworld, of darkness and cold, whom he must vanquish to preserve the Fifth Sun, or fifth age, and thereby protect human life.[3] Every day at dawn, exhausted from fighting, Ollintonatiuh is consoled by the *cihuapipiltin*, or women who have died during childbirth and have subsequently been deified because their days ended in struggle, just as those of warriors. These deities could harm humans, making them sick on given days or attacking them at crossroads. To ward off these evils, feasts and rituals were carried out (Garibay K. 1965; León Portilla 1974). The *cihuapipiltin* show the courage that is characteristic of mothers and express the link between reproduction and divinity that is frequently found in agrarian-based cultures.

In the Valley of Mexico, burials, which date from the dawn of the preclassic period (approximately 1500 B.C. to A.D. 300), point to a clear association between motherhood and agriculture, with the principal deity being Mother Earth. The dead were placed in a fetal position, facing east, the direction of the rising sun, surrounded by food and their prized possessions, such as the clay figurines that have been called "mujeres bonitas" (pretty women). These figurines show an exaltation of the hips as a sexual attribute as well as of hairstyles, adornments, and tattoos that will be maintained until the postclassic period.

As the culture assumed greater ritualistic and military overtones, artistic representations gradually moved away from naturalism and became laden with symbolism until they lost nearly every connection with our notion of the human figure. Coatlicue's gender is barely distinguishable; what is significant is that she is a goddess and as such must instill respect and fear and distance herself from human women, who are burdened by a patriarchal society.

This duality fully expresses the distance that existed between myth and reality. Women always depended on men, whether the latter were their fathers or husbands, even though women had a specific role in production, in accordance with a division of labor that assigned them domestic chores. These chores included not only cleaning and cooking but also preparing *nixtamal* (cooked or limed corn) for tortillas, spinning, weaving, sewing, making ceramics, and carrying out some specific tasks related to agriculture and animal domestication.

Although some authors (Garza Tarazona 1991; Ojeda and Rossell 1995) suggest that women of noble birth were able to occupy positions in the priesthood or the military, few indications support this claim. We need only recall the exclamation made by Friar Toribio de Motolinía, the devout evangelist of the Indians: "It appears that they wanted [women] to be blind, deaf and mute" (quoted in Rodríguez 1987, 29). That a sixteenth-century Spanish friar would be bewildered by the requirements imposed on women is telling.

The construction of gender began at birth: a girl's umbilical cord was buried under the hearth of the home, whereas a boy's was buried in the patio or field, symbolizing the free life that he was to lead. The toys children played with also hinted at their future life: girls were given small brooms for sweeping or small pots for cooking, in contrast with the toy farming tools or weapons that were presented to boys.

Women in Social Organization

Mexica culture was sustained to a large degree by corn farming. Land belonged, originally, to the monarch (*tlatoani*), but it was lent in usufruct to the plebeians (*macehualtin*), who worked it in communes (*calpulli*) or under the administration of the nobles (*pipiltin*). Although it has been speculated that some women may have been landowners (*cihuatlalli*), the topic has not been sufficiently researched for us to arrive at a definitive conclusion. What appears certain, however, is that the *calpulli*[4] communally farmed a parcel of land in order to feed widows and orphans; thus, society ensured the survival of its weakest groups. Whereas in the *calpulli*, endogamy was preferred, among the *pipiltin*, exogamy was the most accepted form of marriage. The leading nobles, who could provide for several women, practiced polygamy. They were allowed to have a first, or original, wife, in addition to several principal wives, concubines, and slaves—all of whom, along with their offspring, had the rights and the status conferred by legitimacy.

At the pinnacle of theocratic rule was the *tlatoani*, who represented the ruling class. Government exerted an inexorable control and was centralized in a complex state apparatus that regulated all economic and ideological activities and rigidly determined the division of social strata as well as work methods and schedules. Social mobility was nearly nonexistent.

Education was obligatory. Schools were set aside for each social class: *pipiltin* boys attended the Calmecac, young *macehualtin* studied at the Telpochcalli. Girls were educated in domestic responsibilities and religion by their mothers, in accordance with their specific social class: the daughters of nobles were taught in a section of the Calmecac and were instructed in health and first aid. Life was considered a difficult passage in which "our Lord gave us laughter and sleep, and the food and drink with which we grow up and live; he also gave us the office of procreation, with which we multiply in the world; all these things give some happiness in our lives for a short time" (Sahagún 1956, 126).

Sexuality was linked to religion and considered to be of divine origin, if of earthly nature, and it appears to have been well accepted within marriage (Quezada 1994; Tuñón Pablos 1991). Still, Spanish sources convey the idea that the Mexicas considered sex an element of human pleasure and a threat to the precarious balance between the individual, society, and the universe and consequently felt it must be controlled within precise limits so as not to violate the cosmic order. In *Historia de las cosas de Nueva España*, Bernardino de Sahagún conveys, through his informants, the beliefs and daily life of the Indians just after the conquest as well as much about how Mexica women lived. He also records much of the advice that was given to the daughters of the nobility and provides us with insight into the social morality of the era. By emphasizing some of the norms, he informs us of the most frequent violations thereof. Nevertheless, we must keep in mind that the social morality considered valid is often that of the upper classes; this morality is subsequently transmitted to the less privileged.

Women were advised to pray frequently, particularly at night, because this practice pleased the gods:

> Be sure, daughter, to rise at night and to keep vigil and to stand
> with your arms outstretched; promptly put on your clothes,
> wash your face, wash your hands, wash your mouth, and
> promptly take the broom to sweep, sweep with diligence, do not

lie idly in bed; rise and wash the mouths of the gods and offer
them incense, and be careful, do not stop [doing] this out of
sloth. . . . Once this is done, begin forthwith to do that which is
your office, or to make cocoa, or to grind corn, or to spin, or to
weave; be careful that you learn very well how food and drink
are made, so that [they] will be made correctly; learn very well
to make good food and good drink, which is called delicate food
and drink for noblemen . . . , and be careful to learn with much
diligence and all curiosity and attention how this food and drink
is made, since in this manner you will be honored and loved and
enriched, wherever god might give you the fate of your marriage.
(Sahagún 1956, vol. 2, bk. 6, ch. 18, 126)

The daily life of Mexica men and women was controlled down to the
smallest details. It was believed that, "[h]ere in this world we are
traveling on a very narrow and very high and very dangerous path . . .
[above] great profundity and depth, without ground [below] and if you
should stray away from the path . . . you will fall into that great depth.
Therefore, it is advisable to stay on the path with great caution. Very
tenderly beloved daughter of mine, beloved little dove, keep this example in your heart" (ch. 19, 134), for "in this world there is no true
pleasure, nor true rest; rather, there are work and afflictions and extreme
weariness, and an abundance of misfortunes and poverties" (ch. 18, 126).
   Women had to comply with social norms, for their own happiness and
well-being, "[so that] you may live in a world of peace and with rest and
contentment [during] those days when you live" (ch. 19, 135). Since
women were an integral part of a group that had not taken the concept
of individualism to its extremes and that placed individuals along a
family line in which deviations would have negative consequences for
their ancestors, their behavior had to reflect their respect for tradition.
The mother said, "Be sure not to sully the honor and fame of our
forebears from whom you come; be sure to honor me and your father and
to give us fame with your good life" (ch. 19, 135). Similarly, these norms
were to be transmitted to one's descendants: "With these same words
you must teach your sons and daughters, if god should give you [any]"
(ch. 11, 132). Clearly, individualism was perilous; the individual formed
part of a larger group, "because you did not make yourself, nor did you
form yourself; your mother and I had that care and we made you, because
this is the custom in the world; it is not an invention of anyone; it is the
arrangement [made by] our god so that there will be engendering through
man and woman" (ch. 18, 129). In this way, Sahagún avoided the topic
of pleasure as a motivation for sexuality.
   Advice was given first by the father, as the spokesman of his society,

and then the mother reasserted what he said: "The first task that I give you is that you keep and that you not forget what your lord and father already said, because these are all very precious things" (ch. 19, 132). In describing a patriarchal system in which the progenitor conferred social status, the mother said, "your beloved father knows that you are his daughter, begotten by him; you are his blood and his flesh and god our lord knows this is so, even though you are a woman, an image of your father" (ch. 19, 132). The father also advised his daughter to respect her mother, "from whose womb you came, like a stone that is cut from another, and she begot you like a [blade of] grass that begets another; in this manner you sprang forth and were born of your mother" (ch. 18, 127).

Although it was felt that both the father and mother had conceived their daughter, the woman's role appears to be acknowledged specifically in child-rearing as well. The mother asks her daughter to "notice that I love you much, [since] you are my beloved daughter; remember that I carried you in my womb for nine months; and ever since you were born, you grew up in my arms: I would put you in your crib and from there on my lap, and with my milk I nursed you" (ch. 19, 132). The mother nurtured and cared for her, but she assumes the role of the spokeswoman for the code of social conduct: "[W]hat else can you hear [besides] what you have heard from your lord and father?" (ch. 19, 132).

Mexican society was clearly patriarchal, although traditions alluding to matrilineal forms of existence were present; for example, the succession of the *tlatoani* took into account the female lineage: Ilancuéitl was the woman who transmitted to the Mexicas the lineage of the Toltecs of Colhuacán, allowing the ruling house to claim ascendancy from the god Quetzalcóatl. Nevertheless, in everyday life *pipiltin* woman experienced the loss of this symbolic power. Their work was centered around the weaving of blankets and the production of children for their master. Matriarchy does not appear to have existed in the pre-Hispanic world, except in the fantasies of the conquistadors, so avid to find Amazons.

Women's lives were limited in every aspect of their behavior and appearance. And appearance obviously determined the collective opinion of a society in which individuality and privacy did not have the importance and value that they have today; it unavoidably expressed a way of being. Hence, the manner of speaking,[5] walking,[6] and controlling one's gesture,[7] and the words one chose,[8] were conditioned. Women refined an image that would not arouse the curiosity of others: the highest praise a person could receive was the silence provoked by neutral attitudes. Personal appearance needed to conform to these expectations: "Be sure that your dresses are modest and appropriate; be sure that you do not dress up with strange and overly worked things, because this signifies fantasy and a lack of brains, and madness. . . . Nor [should] your dress be very despicable, or dirty or torn, as is that of low people . . . [but rather, it should be] modest and clean, so that you will appear neither fantastic nor despicable" (ch. 19, 132).

Dress clearly showed others, especially a suitor or husband, what type of person one was: "So that your husband will not loathe you, attire yourself, wash yourself and wash your clothes, and may this be [according to] rule[s] and with discretion, because if each day you wash yourself and wash your clothes, it shall be said of you that you are very clean and that you are extremely delightful" (ch. 19, 133–144).

Excessive concern over one's appearance denoted a social role: "may it never happen that you shave your face or put colors on it or on your mouth in order to have a good appearance, because that is a sign of worldly and carnal women . . . the shameless women who have already lost their shame and even their mind and who go around [as if they were] mad and drunk do so; they are called harlots" (ch. 19, 133).

Women wore *huipiles* and *nahuas*; their footwear consisted of *huaraches*; and they kept warm with rebozos;[9] even today indigenous women and women of the popular classes use rebozos to carry their youngest children, and many also continue to braid their hair.

Female deities, by contrast, were depicted adorned with jewels, necklaces or pectorals, gold and jade earpieces, lip rings made of precious stones, and headdresses. These deities represent women as a photograph negative might, and, to this extent, they are revealing of a society, of its deepest fears and of its realities.

The Fear of Sexuality: "Do Not Give Your Body to Anyone"

Defined by their biology in a patriarchal society whose deities express the inescapable attraction exerted by their reproductive capacity, women naturally suffered a precise, strict regulation of their sexuality. The first law in the set of norms accounted for in the Spanish sources is summarized as follows: "[D]o not give your body to anyone; be sure you guard yourself closely so that no one will come to you, no one will take your body" (ch. 19, 134). The reason for this appears to have not only moral but practical considerations as well, since if a women were to lose her virginity and later marry, her husband would never forgive her: "And this will be the cause for much affliction and work; you will never be in peace; your husband will always be suspicious of you" (ch. 19, 134). For this reason it was important that "under no circumstance more than one man know you" (ch. 19, 134). In his advice, the father appears more moralistic than practical: "Be careful not to surrender yourself to carnal pleasure; be careful not to throw yourself on the manure and stench of lust; and if you are to come to this, it would be best that you die immediately" (ch. 18, 130).

The preceding quotes hint at a basic fear: that negligence might cause, and be caused, by sexual attraction, for which it was important to neutralize instinct and pleasure. The father also advises his daughter "not to choose among men the one who looks the best to you, as do those who go to buy blankets at the *tianguis* or market; receive he who asks for you, and be careful not to do as one does when growing green corn, which are *xilotes* or *elotes*, [when one] looks for the best and most delicious; be careful not to desire a man because he is the most handsome; be careful not to fall passionately in love with him" (ch. 18, 130). A woman was expected to submissively accept the husband whom her parents had sought through *cihualtianque,* or matchmakers. There were forms of trial marriage, and divorce or repudiation was accepted.

Dedication to marriage was considered a definition of women's lives; their role was established as follows: "When god sees fit for you to take a husband [and once you] are in his possession, be careful not to become haughty, be on guard not to become arrogant, be careful not to degrade yourself, be careful not to give your heart permission to lean elsewhere" (ch. 19, 134–135). Men could have several women, provided that they give them sustenance and care for them; therefore, only the economically privileged could afford to do so. This privilege may also have been granted to warriors who distinguished themselves in combat. Polygamy did not subvert the social order in the same way that adultery committed by women clearly could have. The purpose of this system was to ensure the paternal filiation with children; hence, sexual relations between a married man and single women were not a crime (López Austin 1982, 160). Daughters were advised repeatedly to avoid the "treason known as adultery . . . [because] this, very beloved daughter of mine, is a fall into a bottomless abyss for which there is no remedy; nor can it be cured, in accordance with the practice of the world" (Sahagún 1956, vol. 2, bk. 6, ch. 18, 135). The punishment for women who committed such a transgression was to be cast out from society so that others would be warned, and this punishment was applied to the entire family lineage.[10] It was believed that even if the occurrence did not become publicly known, the gods would learn of it because nothing could escape their attention, and the punishment would bring down manifold misfortunes and much evil on the sinner.[11] Adultery by married women was punished by death by stoning. This punishment was given to Chalchiuhnetzin, the principal wife of Nezahualpitzintli, and an ongoing war was interrupted so that everyone, men and women alike, could watch the execution.[12] Homosexuality and abortion were also punished harshly.

Such emphasis reveals a fear of unbridled sexuality. *Pipiltin* men, even those married, were also advised regarding the virtue of temperance and moderation by their fathers, who would frighten them by conjuring up the specter of illness and divine anger or by warning them simply that abuse could lead them to be "like a maguey that has been sucked and then dries up" (Sahagún 1956, vol. 2, bk. 6, ch. 18, 145–146).

Sexual strength was controlled by Tlazolteotl, and rituals and celebrations in his honor included simulations of intercourse. Priests representing some deities took vows of celibacy in order to be more effective in their activities. We know of the case of Ce Acatl Topiltzin Quetzalcóatl, who was forced to leave Tula, the city he governed, after he was overwhelmed by the shame of becoming inebriated and breaking his vow of sexual abstinence. There appears to have been more tolerance toward plebeians, as indicated in the norms established in the Calmecac and the Telpochalli, which even permitted carnal relations with "maidens" (López Austin 1982, 155). It is clear that the ruling groups were expected to expend all their energy on governing rather than on worldly pleasure. Nevertheless, as Pilar Gonzalbo (1987b, 34) has pointed out, "[t]he rigor of the moral norms [that were] applied to both sexes expressed an ideal behavior and not necessarily one that was systematically observed in all cases."[13]

Desire is portrayed as a force that is unlikely to be subdued, which explains both the insistence on advice of this type as well as the affectionate tone with which warnings are given regarding something that is more dangerous than it appears and the disregard of which will bring about limitless pain. From the pieces of advice brought together by Sahagún, we infer the idea of the overwhelming force of female sexuality. For this reason males are cautioned to be temperate so that they will not expend their strength and thus earn the contempt of their wives: "Your wife will do to you thusly, because, since you are already dry and have nothing to give her, you say to her ['] I cannot any more[']; she will loathe you and discard you, because you do not satisfy her desire and she will seek another because you are now exhausted; and even if she did not already have such a thought, because of the shortcoming she found in you, she will commit adultery against you, and [she will do] so because you destroyed yourself, giving yourself to women, and you exhausted yourself ahead of time" (Sahagún 1956, vol. 2, bk. 6, ch. 18, 145).

Similarly Sahagún relates an anecdote that explains women's ardor: When Netzahualcóyotl was lord of Texcoco, two old women with white hair were detained for having had sexual relations with very young men. The monarch asked them why their desire had not yet been exhausted, to which they answered: "You men when you are old cease wanting carnal pleasure because you had it frequently in your youth, because the potency of human semen comes to an end; we women, however, never tire or become weary of this act, because our body is like an abyss and like a deep ravine that never fills up, it receives everything that is put into it

and desires more and requests more, and if we do not do this, we will not
have life" (ch. 18, 146).

Sahagún speaks to us of the *auanimine*, a Nahuatl word translated as
"the happy woman" or the "woman that gives happiness." Nevertheless, it is clear that a "prostitute" is considered a woman who has lost her
"mind," her human dimension. The Christian viewpoint slights prostitutes' social role, reducing their condition to one of personal vice and
criticizing them for "follow[ing] the path of beasts" (vol. 3, bk. 10, ch. 15,
130). For the Mexicas, however, life options were narrowly determined
by the deity who ruled over one's birth date. One of the few alternatives
for women born under the hegemony of Xochiquetzal was prostitution,
a fate that could be evaded by pursuing activities related to weaving. Free
will was limited: it governed a narrow, although sufficient, range of
choices. The acceptance of one type of life constrained the individual to
a stereotype:

> [A] whore is a public woman and she has the following: she goes
> about selling her body, she begins from an early age and does not
> stop [doing so even] when she is old, and she goes about as [if she
> were] drunk and lost, and she is an elegant and polished woman,
> and with this [she is] very shameless; and she gives herself to
> any man and sells him her body, because she is very lustful,
> dirty and shameless, gossipy, and very debauched in the carnal
> act; she polishes herself much and is so careful in attiring herself
> and she looks like a rose after once she is dressed up, and to em-
> bellish herself she first looks in the mirror, bathes, washes very
> well and she refreshes herself to be more pleasing. She also often
> anoints herself with a yellow earth unguent that she calls *axin*,
> in order to have a good and bright countenance, and sometimes
> she puts colors and embellishment on her countenance, because
> she is lost and worldly. She also has the custom of dying her
> teeth with cochineal and letting her hair down to [look] more
> beautiful . . . and later going around strutting like a shameless,
> dissolute, wicked, vile and bad woman. (ch. 15, 129–130)

Coquetry, then, appears to be the private domain of prostitutes.
Whereas "modest" women were required to maintain discretion, public
women combed their hair in various manners, perfumed themselves
with fragrances. and chewed *tzictli* (gum) to clean their teeth. In
addition, they laughed openly, strolled, and looked for men in the street
(ch. 15, 130).

Even if we assume that the social morality described above in fact regulated the behavior of the different social classes, Mexican society was governed by a gender-based set of norms in accordance with a rigid structure in which each social class's virtues and shortcomings were stipulated. Sahagún applies Spanish titles to indigenous hierarchies, and therefore speaks of "hidalgas" (minor noble women) and "doncellas" (maidens); however, beyond this, he gives us an approximation of social expectations. Hence, a "noble woman is very esteemed, worthy of honor and reverence, and, because of her virtue and nobility in everything, gives favor to and protects those who come to her; and such [a woman], if she is good, has these qualities, such that under her wings the poor, [whom] she loves and treats very well, are protected; and if she is not such, she is passionate, callous, she does not have any consideration for others and she is haughty and presumptuous" (ch. 13, 124). Her gender role as a mother extends to the dispossessed, in strict accordance with a top-down system of government that openly used paternalistic principles to maintain power, and that would eventually influence the figure of Guadalupe.

Sahagún also tells us of women who wove, sewed, and cooked, and of women doctors who delivered infants and cured physical ailments with herbs and rituals. He describes how pre-Hispanic women took part in society, on the basis of the specificity determined by their biology but also in accordance with their particular social group. In a myth allusive to the imminence of conquest, their role acquired the basic meaning of motherhood, which, as a gender, women in all social classes shared. Indigenous testimonies report that this fateful event was presaged by a series of premonitions: fire rained on the city of Tenochtitlán, water boiled, the temple of Huitzilopochtli burned, a comet shot across the sky, and "many times we heard a woman crying; she was screaming during the night; she was making loud shrieks: 'Little children of mine, we now have to go far away!' And at times she would say, '[l]ittle children, where shall I take you?'" (León Portilla 1972, 4).

The legend of *la llorona* emerged from the ambiguous figure of the *cihuapipiltin*, women who died in their first childbirth and who were deified, but who returned to earth on certain dates to do harm. This legend could also refer to the goddess Cihuacóatl, a variation of the goddess Tonantzin, who was associated with the serpent woman who brought destruction and work to humans and at night "cried and wailed in the air" (Sahagún 1956, vol. 1, bk. 1, ch. 6, 46). (Sahagún assumed that this was a version of Eve in the Christian tradition, "since they had news of the [event] that occurred between our mother Eve and the serpent" [ch. 6, 46].)

The legend of *la llorona* still frightens Mexican children when at night they have any premonition of misfortune.

2

Women in New Spain
The End of One World and
the Shaping of Another

෪෪

What the indigenous people of Mexico experienced as the catastrophe that ended their world was a process that opened the way to a different reality. The Spanish Conquest pitted two worlds against each other—both powerful, both going through political and military expansion, both deeply religious, and both characterized by a patriarchal or male-dominated system.

Nonetheless, despite their similarities, the two cultures were fundamentally different: The native peoples of Mexico believed in a cyclical concept of time in which events were thought to be predetermined and otherness was often made homologous to one's own perspective, as part of the collective identity expressed through ritual and symbolism. The Spaniards, in contrast, had a linear concept of time that projected toward the future. They strongly emphasized individualism, probably as a result of the Christian concept of "free will," and they perceived "the other" as a threat and tried to destroy it (Todorov 1987). These differences took on special importance in the two cultures' different technological capabilities: the gunpowder used in Spanish harquebuses and cannons, compared to the bow and arrow of the natives, gave the new arrivals an enormous advantage.

Hernán Cortés arrived on the eastern coast of Mexico in 1519 and conquered the city of México-Tenochtitlán in 1521. During the first years of Spanish rule, internal power struggles were fierce. In 1535, with the creation of the viceroyalty, conflicts were tempered and conditions were created to slowly transform the Mesoamerican territory into New Spain and integrate it into the world capitalist system, within which it was assigned the role of supplier of minerals. Over the three centuries that the colonial period lasted, the Spaniards expanded their presence throughout Aridamerica by sending military and religious advance parties. They reached as far as the present-day U.S. states of Texas, California, Arizona, and New Mexico, although their presence in these regions was minimal.

This new organization meant not that indigenous lifestyles were completely forgotten, but rather that autochthonous practices gradually lost currency and were integrated into mestizo and criollo forms of organization, eventually constituting a new system. Change existed alongside continuity; traditions, customs, and popular beliefs were preserved—elements which, as Pilar Gonzalbo (1987b, 44) notes, "the victors did not give importance [to nor] judge dangerous. . . . Indigenous women were the main vehicle for the transmission of those traditional ways of thinking, which were reflected both in attitudes toward life and in seemingly trivial routines, in contrast with the permanent concern regarding dogma and orthodoxy."

The Spanish project for the new territories was determined by the economic system that prevailed in Europe. Spain was obliged to obtain precious metals so as to have access to the capitalist system: the colonies supplied gold and silver to a core region that needed them in order to establish ties with nations that, however recently, had introduced manufacturing and were already on the road to global economic domination. That these territories were integrated into the West from a position of dependency and as suppliers of raw materials would determine their historical development.

Nevertheless, as was the case elsewhere, capitalism did not develop in a pure or homogeneous manner. Pre-Columbian economic and social practices were preserved to an important extent, although more in some regions than in others; consequently, they coexisted with both the practices of the emerging capitalist system and the remnants of the feudal system that the conquistadors had brought with them. The conquest signified the destruction of one world while it created the technical and economic possibilities that would incorporate Mexico into the global capitalist system, although from a position of dependency. This was mercantile capitalism, since the sugar mills and *obrajes* (textile mills) never constituted full-fledged industries. Moreover, New Spain supplied agricultural products not to the core region but only to the internal market; hence, in the shadow of imperial rule, a social group that prospered from the needs of the colony was created.

Agricultural production had to be modified in accordance with the pronounced demographic changes: 90 percent of the indigenous population died in the sixteenth century, and Spanish settlers continued to arrive throughout the colonial period, leading to the growth of the mestizo and criollo populations. Although the *encomienda*[1] system initially provided the Spaniards with the labor they needed for the colony's survival, this labor soon proved insufficient and became a justification for grouping the indigenous population into communities in which, though their form of communal landholding was at times respected, more often their lands were stripped from them and they were controlled in accordance with a specific set of norms. The need to supply the central and northern areas of the country brought about the creation of the hacienda, which would survive until the twentieth century. This form of private ownership of land and of agricultural and livestock production expanded at the expense of the indigenous communities, notwithstanding the Crown's support for Indian rights as a way of curbing the settlers' ambitions. Indians who refused to assimilate were marginalized and became increasingly vulnerable.

Modes of production were largely determined by the spatial distribution of people. In areas with the greatest criollo influence (Bajío, an area that includes Guanajuato and Michoacán; and the north), a predominantly capitalist economy developed, whereas in those with the highest concentration of Indians (the center and the south), pre-Hispanic elements such as communal landholding survived. The north was sparsely populated, and colonization arrived there late and advanced slowly: New Mexico was colonized in the sixteenth century,[2] Texas in the seventeenth century, and California not until the eighteenth century.

The white population concentrated in the cities. In 1670, approximately 57 percent of the criollo population lived in ten cities. The social hierarchy was based on skin color, which, along with surname and rank, determined one's social position. Over the course of three centuries, criteria based on color partially gave way to criteria of an economic nature; thus, impoverished whites could also be found. The racial melting pot of New Spain gradually fused together the different shades of colors. Mestizos, who would interbreed with *castas*, or persons of mixed race, became the predominant racial group.[3] Women were an integral part of this process. Gradual miscegenation meant that African influence ceased to be evident. Asunción Lavrin (1978, 14) points out that "urban nonwhite women readily adopted many traits of the Spanish culture as they became affluent. Social climbing and acculturation obliterated racial differences in lifestyles and patterns of behavior."

In the aftermath of the conquest, Indians lost to the dominant system the differences and nuances characteristic of a multifaceted culture, as the different groups were lumped together in the category of the vanquished and subordinated. Importantly, not until 1537 did Pope Paul III declare that Indians possess a soul, thereby granting them human status. Whites held positions of privilege in every domain, and people of mixed race gradually became the largest population group. This miscegenation was carried out freely by the actors, both men and women—notwithstanding the Crown's uncertain attempts to prevent it.

Marina: Symbol of *Mestizaje*

Spain also suffered from deep social and cultural contradictions, which were reflected in the concept of women, a concept based on the ingrained belief in the inferiority of women but also influenced by Christian ambivalence and the perception that sexual pleasure was inherently evil as well as a sign of animality and sin. In addition, all of this was filtered through the military and religious aggrandizement of the "Reconquista," or expulsion of the Arabs, and by the chivalrous image of Amadis of Gaul, of whom, Bernal Díaz del Castillo said, "they [the Spanish conquerors] all believed they had a little." The new arrivals came laden with legends, some of which revolved around women. The best known, the legend of the Amazons, can be traced back to Greek culture. It alluded to women warriors who only occasionally had sexual relations, and then solely for procreating. The search for the Amazons conjured up fantasies in the minds of Spaniards, who frequently thought that they had found them.

Most of the Spaniards who volunteered for this new undertaking were either single or had left their wives safely protected on the Iberian Peninsula. Few Spanish women came to the New World in the first years, and those who did come generally settled in the islands that had already been colonized. Between 1509 and 1538, 10 percent of the boarding permits issued by the Casa de Contratación (House of Trade) in Seville were granted to married women who hoped to rejoin their husbands in the New World; most of these women, however, would end up swelling the ranks of convents and brothels (Moreno Toscano 1981, 1:321). It was natural that concubinage would emerge almost immediately.

Indigenous women were present from the beginning of the war of conquest: among the first gifts Cortés received from Moctezuma was a group of women slaves for his delight. In both worlds, then, women were objects to be bestowed and with whom to seek pleasure. Bernal Díaz del Castillo recounts that in March 1519, Cortés and his men received presents from the caciques and headmen of Tabasco, from a town they called Santa María de la Victoria, the most important of which were twenty women, including Mallinalitzin (Malinche). He noted that Cortés received this gift with pleasure.

The Spaniards were prohibited from having physical contact with non-Christian women, and the candidates to be their concubines clearly did not meet this requirement. Hence a double standard quickly appeared among these men: given the delay that a normal evangelization process would have entailed, the conquistadors chose to baptize the women quickly. Díaz del Castillo relates that Fray Bartolomé de Olmedo, through Jerónimo de Aguilar's translation, "preached many good things of our holy faith to the twenty Indian women who [had been] given to us and [he exhorted to them] not to believe in the idols in which they previously believed, [adding] that they were bad and they were not gods, [and telling them] to not make sacrifices to them any more, that they had been deceived, and to adore Our Lord Jesus Christ. And they were quickly baptized; . . . these were the first Christian women . . . in New Spain, and Cortés distributed to each captain his own" concubine (Díaz del Castillo 1942, 1:120–121). The recently converted Marina was given to Alonso Hernández Puerto Carrero.

It was natural to present women as gifts in protocolary ceremonies. Díaz del Castillo explains that the caciques of Tlaxcala "brought five Indians, beautiful maidens and girls, and although they were Indians, they were of pleasant appearance and well-dressed, and they brought for each Indian woman another Indian girl for her service, and all were daughters of *caciques*. And Xicotenga said to Cortés: 'Malinche[4] . . . this is my daughter, and she has not married, . . . she is a maiden and take her for yourself.' And she gave Cortés Malinche's hand [in marriage, telling him] to give the others to the captains. And Cortés thanked her . . . with a pleasant expression that showed that he was receiving them and taking them as his" (Díaz del Castillo 1942, 1:23). They were baptized and given to the captains.

The figure of Mallinalitzin-Marina-Malinche stands out as the symbol of this process of miscegenation that entailed clear subordination. According to Díaz del Castillo, Marina was originally from the area near Coatzacoalcos, on the boundary between areas controlled by the Mayas and Mexicas, where the latter had expanded militarily. She was the daughter of the caciques of Paynalá, and the heir to some land. Her mother, who had married for the second time, sold her to some merchants. This transaction was the first stage of a journey that would take Marina to areas with diverse cultural influences. As a result, she spoke Mayan and Nahuatl and, along with Jerónimo de Aguilar, she was able to bridge the language gap and communicate with Moctezuma's ambassadors. Her gift for learning languages allowed her to learn Spanish, and for this reason she was given a leading role among the troops of the Conquistador. When the indigenous emissaries informed Moctezuma of the arrival of the conquistadors, they added that "[a] woman, one of [those of us] who are from here, accompanies them; she comes speaking in the Nahuatl tongue. Her name, Malintzin; her house, Teticpac. Down on the coast they first took her" (León Portilla 1974, 37). The native people came to think of her as Cortés's voice; indeed, they assimilated the two persons to such an extent that they would refer to don Hernán as "Malinche."

Marina has been institutionalized as the symbol of *mestizaje*. Her presence is so strong in the Mexican psyche that some have tried to understand the psychology of Mexicans on the basis of the conflict she arouses. Octavio Paz (1985, 71), for example, has explained the character of the mestizo as follows:

> The character of the Mexican is a product of the social circumstances that prevail in our country, and the history of Mexico, which is the history of these circumstances, contains the answer to every question. The situation that prevailed during the colonial period would thus be the source of our closed, unstable attitude.

Paz further understands that "historical events are something more than events because they are colored by humanity, which is always problematical" (ibid.).

Nevertheless, Marina is a complex figure. For the Spaniard, it was she who "in all the wars of New Spain and Tlaxcala and Mexico was such an excellent woman and [had] a good tongue" (Díaz del Castillo 1942, 1:120). Cortés made her not only his interpreter but his mistress as well, and she bore him a son, Martín, whom Cortés legitimized through a bull issued by Pope Clement VII in 1529. He also made his son a knight of the Order of St. James. When Marina ceased to be useful to Cortés, he married her to one of his soldiers, the hidalgo Juan Jaramillo, with whom she lived in comfort until her death. According to Díaz del Castillo, Marina had said, "even if they made [me] *cacica* of all the provinces there were in New Spain, [I] would not be one, since [I] had more [to do] in serving [my] husband and Cortés than all that there is in the world" (ibid., 1:124).

Malinche is accused of valuing a foreign culture more than her own, of having betrayed Mexico as a country; she is therefore asked to be faithful to a Mexican nation that would not exist as such for another three centuries. Marina had been enslaved by the Mexicas and she allied herself with the enemies of her own enemies, which in a vanquished and sexually rigid society is unforgivable. Essentially she is asked to be faithful to the race that she did not know as such, since she belonged to a people who were enemies of the Mexicas. Nevertheless, it is clear that this demand is made of her in terms of her function as an archetype that surpasses by far her historical persona. She is the symbol of the prevailing sex-gender system, part of that mythology that the national culture insists on exalting, even if it does so by denigrating it. She keeps alive the idea of *mestizaje*, with its sense of social hierarchization.

Another significant case, that of Gonzalo Guerrero, has been overlooked. Guerrero and Jerónimo de Aguilar shipwrecked off the coast of present-day Tabasco. However, Guerrero took a path opposite that of

Aguilar, who refused to integrate into the indigenous community that had given him refuge for seven years and who therefore was marginalized. Guerrero, by contrast, held a prominent position in a nearby village and even married into a leading family. When de Aguilar, who had been made a slave, tried to convince Guerrero to join the new arrivals, Guerrero responded, "I am married and have three children; they consider me a *cacique* and a captain when there are wars; go with God because my face has been furrowed and my ears have been pierced . . . and you see these children of mine, how lovely they are." And Guerrero's wife said furiously, "[l]ook with what [requests] this slave comes and calls my husband; go away and do not heed my words" (ibid., 98). Hence Guerrero remained with the Indians, demonstrating another, different type of *mestizaje* that entailed cultural adaptation.

Although chronologically Guerrero's offspring would be Mexico's first mestizos, the case of Malinche is significant in that it reflects the higher hierarchical position of one social group over another, the subordination of women to a male chieftain on two counts: through conquest and based on gender. Octavio Paz has written that

> Doña Marina becomes a figure representing the Indian women who were fascinated, violated or seduced by the Spaniards. And as a small boy will not forgive his mother if she abandons him to search for his father, the Mexican people have not forgiven La Malinche for her betrayal. She embodies the open, the *chingado*, to our closed, stoic, impassive Indians. (1985, 86)

She represents *Lo chingado*, or that which is opened up, is split apart, is given, and, in the process, is contaminated, broken, and eschewed by others. This feminine principle is associated with the violated mother. In Marina, continues Paz,

> Her passivity is abject: She does not resist violence, but is an inert heap of bones, blood and dust. Her taint is constitutional and resides, as we said earlier, in her sex. This passivity, open to the outside world, causes her to lose her identity: she is the *Chingada*. She loses her name; she is no one; she disappears into nothingness; she *is* Nothingness. And yet she is the cruel incarnation of the feminine condition. (Ibid., 85–86)

For this reason, the insult "*hijo de la chingada*" requires the acceptance that each and every one of us, in our own manner, are sons and daughters of *la chingada*.

The figure of Malinche has been reevaluated in recent years and from different perspectives. Clearly she was a very skillful woman, since her efforts as a translator required her to bridge two mentalities and two worldviews and to take into account distinct political needs. For fifteen months her role was crucial. It is tempting to think that Malinche lied to all, distorting both sides' discourse to avoid war during a one-year period in 1519 and 1520.[5]

For the most part, the Indians did not accept colonization willingly. They resisted in manifold ways. The historical sources suggest how deeply painful the Spanish presence must have been and that women had a role beyond involvement in sexual trade with the conquistadors. There are references to collective suicides, to villages that refused to have children and that committed infanticide or practiced systematic abortion so that their legacy as the vanquished would end with their death (Moreno Toscano 1981, 532). Moreover, excessive work and European diseases, against which the Indians had no antibodies, decimated the population. According to Borah and Cook (quoted in Moreno Toscano 1981, 350), the number of Indians declined from 25.3 million in 1519 to 16.8 million in 1523, 2.6 million in 1548, and 1.3 million in 1595. The white population, by contrast, tended to increase during the entire colonial period, thanks to favorable living conditions and constant immigration.

Guadalupe: Cultural *Mestizaje*

Mestizaje entails more than the physical mixing of cultures; it also refers precisely to a cultural dynamic by which two traditions are integrated. The latter process is succinctly expressed in another feminine symbol: Guadalupe. She symbolizes the syncretism between the Virgin Mary, who was highly esteemed in Spain since the late Middle Ages, and Tonantzin, the goddess-mother of fertility. The Virgin of Guadalupe made herself known to the conquered people through an Indian goatherd, Juan Diego, who observed her saintly appearances in 1531, on Tepeyac Hill, the former sanctuary of the Nahuatl goddess Tonantzin, whom the Mexicas called "our mother." Guadalupe is a dark-skinned virgin whose racial characteristics were very important at the time and who took on the role of patroness of the forsaken. During the colonial period, although she and the Spanish Virgen de los Remedios would alternate as the most prominent religious figures, Guadalupe was the favorite among the popular classes. Importantly, Guadalupe's purely religious meaning later led to nationalist symbolism, to a political design: criollo clerics fomented the veneration of Guadalupe for reasons that probably had as much to do with insurgency as with faith. Upon initiating the movement for independence from Spain in 1810, the "Father of the Nation,"

Miguel Hidalgo, made the image of Guadalupe the standard of freedom, and in her name battles were fought against Guadalupe's rival, the Virgen de los Remedios.

Guadalupe also expresses another feminine myth, one that is somewhat opposed to Marina, although complementary to her. The treacherous woman—the sexed prostitute, who, despite being an Indian, attains Spanish status—confronts the pure religious woman, who, based on Christian faith, cares for her people, even though this meant adopting the religion of the conqueror. The Virgin-Mother is, even today, the repository of the nation's devotion: she watches over her sons and daughters, although she excludes sexual meaning from all procreation.

Mestizaje as expressed by Guadalupe occurred in New Spain in those first years: to reach the indigenous population, the church made genuine attempts to adapt its rituals. At the height of the evangelization process (until about 1570), it experimented with various methods to entice the Indians to accept Christianity as the ideological vehicle of Spanish domination and as the expression of the culture of empire. To bring about a rapid catechization, the faith was adapted to indigenous rituals; for example, mass was celebrated in open spaces, as traditional pre-Hispanic ceremonies of worship had been; methods that used eyesight, hearing, and the sense of smell to transmit the story of Christ were studied; and an attempt was made to reconcile autochthonous beliefs with those of the recently arrived Spaniards. The first result was religious syncretism: Christian symbols—the Cross, for example—were accepted because of their similarity with indigenous icons.

This syncretism is understandable, given the way in which the Spaniards attempted to change Indian thinking. In *Visión de los vencidos*, León Portilla (1972, 62) relates that the first woman to be baptized was Yacotzin, the mother of Ixtlixúchitl, who was one of the headmen of Tezcoco and related to Coancoch, who had supported Cortés and converted to Christianity in 1519. When Ixtlixúchitl tried to convert his mother, "[s]he responded that he must have lost his mind, since he so quickly allowed himself to be won over by a few barbarians as were the Christians. To which Don Hernando [Ixtlixúchitl's Christian name] responded that if she weren't his mother, his response would be to behead her, and that he would have to do so [anyway], even though he did not want to, since it was the life of the soul that mattered" (ibid., 95). Yacotzin tried to win time by offering to think the situation over, but her son set her house on fire, after which she agreed to be baptized, with Hernán Cortés himself acting as her godfather, and she was given the name Doña María.

Women had a basic role in the integration process, as the Crown well understood. As early as 1528 it established schools for indigenous girls, with the express intent that, in adopting the faith, they would serve as an example of adherence to Christian values to those around them. This effort clearly shows the link between evangelization and culture. By the mid–sixteenth century, nine such schools had been established, the first in Tezcoco, and they were administrated by Spanish women who had come to the New World with that specific mission.

Mestizaje, as a process that transcended racial questions, gave birth to one culture through the integration of two others. Hence, the symbols of Marina and Guadalupe depict this process, although they do not fully explain the question of women's integration during this period. How did typical women experience the conquest? How did it affect their daily lives, their daily habits, the way in which they went about their chores, and the meaning the latter had for them? What was women's role during the transition and during the consolidation of the viceroyalty? The answers undoubtedly depend on the social class in question. There is, however, one common element that to a greater or lesser degree affected the situation of women, whether Indians or criollas, religious or lay, urban or rural: gender as defined by a patriarchal society.

The viceroyalty preserved the system of male privilege that it had inherited from each side. Hence the pre-Columbian concept of women seems to have been adapted without further ado to the Christian view: Both cultures centered women's role in marriage and motherhood, and both condemned abortion and sexuality; both considered women's submissiveness, weakness, and devotion to be consubstantial qualities and both idealized virginity; both demonized women who strayed from the path they were expected to follow, considering them violators of both social morality and their "eternal," feminine nature. Nevertheless, there was a tangible difference between actual practice and dominant ideology in this society.

Legal Organization: From Theory to Practice

In the first years, the Spaniards tested the waters. This initial period is generally considered to have lasted until 1535, the year in which the viceroyalty was established, giving authorities in the peninsula greater control. In economic organization, flexibility was maintained for a longer period, since *encomiendas* were normally given for several lifetimes, and the conquistadors' descendants staunchly defended what they considered their birthright. Nevertheless, we cannot view New Spain as a monolith, since tensions existed between the Crown and the *encomenderos*, between newcomers and conquistadors or their descendants, between diocesan priests and those belonging to an order.

For women, the viceroyalty meant social adaptation to a complex system that once again confined them to the familiar environment of the home, this time with the added options of the convent or the public "bawdy house." In studying the situation of women during this period, it is important not to take the historical sources at face value and to remember that, in the colonial system, practice and law were always divorced, as indicated by the well-known formula "to be obeyed but not to be fulfilled" by which royal decrees were obviated. If the law considered women the equals of the men of their race, this was not the case in either regulations or social practice. With Indians, who theoretically were the equals of the Spaniards, the situation was analogous, as it was in the case of colonial territories, which on paper were considered kingdoms like those in Spain, and, consequently, on an equal footing with Castile or León. Notwithstanding the juridical norms, whether civilian or religious, life was conducted in accordance with other, more permissive or flexible rules.

The ethnic breakdown of the population varied greatly over the three centuries that the colonial period lasted. In 1570, 98 percent of the population was indigenous, 0.2 percent was Spanish, and 0.6 percent was black. By 1810, 60 percent of the population was indigenous, 2 percent was Spanish, and the remainder was of mixed race. Regarding the proportion of women within each group, in 1534, for each nine Spanish men who immigrated, only one woman did so. In 1793, only 1.4 percent of all Spaniards in New Spain were women. Roughly half the Indian population was female. It is estimated that around 1773 there were 160,000 black men and only 80,000 black women. The groups showed a palpable tendency to integrate (Tostado 1991, 16–17).

Theoretically, Spaniards, whether *peninsulares* (those born on the Iberian Peninsula) or criollos, held the highest rank in the social hierarchy, followed by Indians, mestizos, *castas,* and blacks. In practice this order was not respected, since the marginalization of Indians meant that they were relegated to the lowest rung. Hence, Spaniards held the highest position, followed by criollos, mestizos, *castas,* and, finally, Indians. Mestizos and *castas* had the advantage of participating more actively in society and of being more familiar with cultural practices (Mörner 1974, 32). Moreover, criteria for racial definition were not very precise. Priests lacked an exact guideline for determining race, and since whites had a higher status, Indians would often state that they were Spaniards or mestizos to circumvent the payment of tributes.

The Crown was especially interested in encouraging marriage to populate the new lands, particularly because the sixteenth-century decline in population had limited the available labor. This was to be carried out in accordance with the law of God and the needs of the kingdom; hence, the achievement of this goal was often incompatible with existing conditions. Cohabitation was common, even though the church's opposition was expressed at every meeting of the Mexican hierarchy (Malvido 1990, 115–130), which suggests that the norm was constantly violated. Similarly, no matter how strongly Spain insisted on racial separation—even spatially, through the coinage of the terms "Republic of Indians" and "Republic of Spaniards"—mixed-race unions were frequent. The reason given for this in the initial period was the lack of Spanish women, since the conquest, as a military undertaking, had been carried out essentially by men.

Ots Capdequi (1976, 97) tells us that in 1539 the Crown prohibited women from traveling to New Spain unaccompanied; however, the acceptance or rejection of their petitions was not decided casuistically. A 1554 royal letter ordered officials of the House of Trade in Seville to see that "women be obliged to provide information on their cleanliness, as men [must do], and not to let any [women] through without express permission"; it also prohibited the departure of gypsies and persons of "loose morals." This clear attempt to prevent prostitution failed: regulations governing this practice were decreed in 1526 on the island of Hispaniola (Santo Domingo), since it was deemed a necessary evil. Much emphasis was placed on the need to preserve marriage ties or to encourage marriage among people who were not formally married. Starting in 1539, married Spaniards were required to bring their wives, and those who were single were required to marry, under penalty of losing their *encomienda* (Mörner 1974, 26). The insistence on this norm suggests its frequent transgression.

Nevertheless, we find that soon afterward white women married men of their own race with the express purpose of maintaining the colonial hierarchy through reproduction. On this point, Rosario Castellanos says:

> the wife, [who had] come from beyond "the briny sea," enjoyed the questionable privileges of legitimacy and gradually became acclimated to these lands where the lord and master was so absolute that he would even forget the forms of courtesy and the norms of treatment in effect in the metropolis, and she would be obliged to descend from her pedestal as a lady (so laboriously built by Castilian women and troubadours in the eighteenth century) to become the fertile bearer of those who would inherit the vast *encomiendas,* the increasingly long surnames, the titles of nobility, the projects that could not be carried out in the term of one generation, the ambitions, the dominions, the riches, the power. (1973, 26)

The legislation of the period classified Spanish married women as minors, and, although they could inherit property, titles, and businesses, their legal rights were subsumed in their marital bonds, and their husband was the administrator of their property. Prior to marriage, they depended on their father or guardian. Reaching legal adulthood, which was twenty-five years of age, afforded them only relative freedom.

Their true milieu was within the family and in the home. Nevertheless, there was some margin for ambiguity. Lawsuits brought by women who had inherited *encomienda* rights for several lifetimes were normally resolved in their favor, and even though these rights might later be annulled (Ots Capdequi 1976, 108–110), it was still common for women to inherit them from husbands and fathers. Ots Capdequi (1976, 104–112) suggests that widowhood allowed women to exercise full legal powers, including custody of their children. The Crown assumed a protective attitude toward widows to avoid their swelling the ranks of the brothels. Hence, a peculiar situation arose: while married, women were subordinated; when widowed, they had rights and received protection. The mother of Juana de Asbaje y Ramírez (Sor Juana Inés de la Cruz), Isabel Ramírez de Santillana, was able to administrate a hacienda that had been rented to her father for three lifetimes, and she even managed to bequeath it to her granddaughter. Some women were teachers in the artisans' guilds and had an active role in business. Still, norms for women's participation in public life were not clear, which suggests that cases were resolved casuistically. It is clear, however, that laws governing women were frequently overlooked for the sake of greater flexibility.

Indians were considered the equals of Spaniards—a distinction not afforded to either blacks or *castas*. The polemic between Bartolomé de las Casas and Ginés de Sepúlveda, who had raised the issue of Indians' legal status, had once again been resolved through the divorce of practice and law. De las Casas successfully argued that Indians be granted the legal status of minors, that is, potential human beings under the protection of Christians to bring their humanity to fruition. Ginés, however, won in practice: Indians were treated as slaves by nature. Because they were theoretically minors, Indians did not pay tithes or sales tax (*alcabala*), nor were they obliged to serve in the military. They did, however, have to pay tributes and render forced labor. They were denied the right to ride horses, use firearms or swords, sign contracts, or buy wine. The indigenous nobility maintained a position of privilege, as a special concession by the conquerors to the vanquished. Indian women were legally equal to men and hence paid tribute. Still, we can imagine that in practice they were oppressed on three fronts: gender, race, and class. They continued to don the *huipil, enaguas* (petticoats), and rebozo, and to braid their hair. Some portrayals show them with uncovered breasts. Their work was related to the home, and it included field work, the making of handcrafts, and house chores, and they also worked as servants in Spanish homes.

Indigenous noblewomen assimilated with their rulers and enjoyed multiple privileges. Isabel Moctezuma, for example, after being widowed by Cuitláhuac and Cuauhtémoc, married a Spaniard and lived in luxury, surrounded by silk and jewels. She was afforded the privilege of wearing Spanish dress, whereas her plebeian counterparts were strictly forbidden to do so. Women from the indigenous nobility were also allowed to use their family's coat of arms and were exempt from paying tribute to the king, although they did have to exact this tax from the inhabitants of the lands they owned.[6]

For Indians, marriage was a difficult step to take, since for some (caciques) it implied passage from a polygynous system to a monogamous one and, especially, a different concept of marriage ties, since Christian unions were indissoluble. Hence, their adaptation to what were deemed moral norms was difficult. The lower classes were reluctant to abide by the practices and customs being imposed on them. *Encomenderos* were prohibited from separating indigenous couples or from employing married women as servants without also taking on their husbands. It is clear, however, that this norm was frequently ignored. The incorporation of the Indians into Spanish social morality was a challenging task. For instance, how should the matter of men with several wives be dealt with? Because of the obligation to choose just one, many women were left without any specific social function. Concubinage represented another hurdle. Clearly this was a thorny issue for Indians and Spaniards alike, and the problem later become one of how to deal with illegitimate children, which led to the frequent abandonment of offspring. The church was then given part of the responsibility of child rearing, which it accepted as a way to avoid filicide, which was also common (Malvido 1990, 123–124). Indigenous men of noble lineage defended their right to have more than one wife, pointing to the benefit created by more weaving (Romero 1991, 35–42). We must remember that indigenous noblewomen produced both children and cloth for their masters. Pilar Gonzalbo (1987b, 44) notes that "colonial laws, which eliminated the obligation and the right to have several families simultaneously, were unable to prevent men from [doing so] secretly and, now, without the responsibility of supporting them."

Concubinage between Spanish men and indigenous women existed alongside legal marriage. Rosario Castellanos (1973, 26) points out that "the Indian concubine was treated as a domestic animal and as [such] was discarded when she ceased to be useful. Regarding the bastards she gave birth to, they were brought up as servants of the main house."

Sometimes, however, these mestizos would wander between Indian and Spanish towns. As early as 1533, the authorities appeared to be deeply troubled by this situation (Mörner 1974, 85). The term *mestizo* was first identified with illegitimacy (ibid., 61), although many mestizos were the offspring of legitimate marriages. These children were deemed Spaniards, since, as noted, precision in terms was in short supply.[7] At the beginning of the viceroyal period, the authorities felt that mixed marriages should be encouraged; this policy, however, quickly changed, as expressed in the popular saying that advised each person to "marry and form godparental ties with his equal."

During the colonial period, the duties and work of mestizas varied, largely in accordance with the region where they lived or the position their family occupied in the production of goods. In cities and villages, they provided services, sold food, and worked as servants in large Spanish houses; in the countryside, they were given domestic and agricultural work. Their dress was simple: it consisted of a shirt, skirt, slip, and shawl, and it took the most comfortable elements from the attire of each social group.

Blacks were deemed to have vile blood; their status as slaves was transmitted by the mother. They were given the most thankless and dangerous tasks. The Crown tried to ensure that they marry only among their own group (Mörner 1974, 77) to keep them in their economic and political status. In the mid–sixteenth century, black males who had sexual relations with women of another race were punished with castration (ibid., 28). Nevertheless, interracial sexual relations were common, since this practice made it possible to initiate the formalities required for emancipation; hence, blacks used their sexual attraction as an instrument to gain liberation (Cortés 1982, 292): black men would seek out Indian women, whereas black women would look for Spanish men, since no one else had the economic means to buy blacks their freedom. In this context, legends flourished. Such is the case of "the mulata of Córdoba," a slave and a sorceress who, according to tradition, was tried by the Inquisition. When she felt her life in peril, she resorted to an ingenious method to get away: She drew a small boat on the wall, got in it, and sailed away over the sea.[8]

Dress laws were rigid. A 1582 statute prohibited black women as well as *mulatas* and mestizas from using indigenous dress unless they were married to an Indian (Cortés 1982, 290). As early as 1571, attempts were made to prevent black women from dressing luxuriously. They were banned from wearing gold, pearls, silk, or other luxury goods available to them through their dealings with Spaniards. If they were married to a Spaniard, they could wear gold earrings with pearls and necklaces, and their skirts could have velvet trimmings. They were prohibited from wearing cloaks, and, instead, were allowed to wear only a mantilla.

Nevertheless, Thomas Gage, an early-seventeenth-century English traveler who came to New Spain while on his way to the Philippines and devoted much time to becoming familiar with the country, expressed surprise at the attire worn by black women, which suggests that the law was not always obeyed. He writes, "Not one goes out without her necklace and pearl bracelet or wristlet, and her earring with some precious stone. The clothes and attire of blacks and mulatas are so lascivious, and their gestures and grace [are] so charming, that many Spaniards, even among those of the upper class—already inclined to lust—leave their wives for them" (Gage 1982, 180).

After describing the attire of silks, fabrics from Holland or China, belts with precious stones, head coverings with letters embroidered in gold, and mantillas made of linen or cambric, he explains that "most of those young women are or have been slaves, and love has given them the freedom to shackle souls and attach them to the yoke of sin and the devil" (Gage 1982, 180).

Oriental presence, as well, was felt in traditions and legends. One such case is the *china poblana* (Chinese woman from Puebla), whom some have identified as a seventeenth-century mystic from Puebla, and others as a Filipino slave who was brought on a ship from China to Mexico. Her lavish attire, inspired by the dress of the Andulusian *maja* or the *lagarterana*, consisted of a broad, bright-colored skirt, embroidered with sequins, a low-necked blouse, and a shawl. It was adapted for everyday use and has now become a regional costume that, along with the *charro* suit worn by men, is today a symbol of Mexicanness.[9]

Although social and racial groups were supposedly segregated, in houses and kitchens, in medicine, in the symbolic treatment of many human problems through sorcery, the links were already forming a common culture.

We can conclude that laws, while rigid in theory, often had to bend in practice. Women's daily lives were governed by their race and gender, and also by their class. What was "supposed to be" failed to conform to the overwhelming reality of desire, vanity, pleasure, and longing for freedom. With some difficulty, women learned to function with ambiguity and to seek spaces in which they could fulfill their own desires, vanities, and pleasures; they also learned to walk the few paths leading to freedom.

The Daily Lives of Women in Streets and Houses—Houses of the Family, Houses of Seclusion, Houses of Prostitution, and Houses of God

Women had an important role in society, and their activities were multiple. Whereas women of the popular classes performed traditional duties, which in the countryside included weaving cloth, making ceramics, and tending to crops, in cities and villages they sold a variety of goods in *tianguis,* or markets, and sometimes they provided social services, such as delivering water. They also were employed as servants for the wealthy. The *Recopilación de Leyes de los Reynos de las Indias* ([1681] 1973), which systematized existing laws, stated that women should not engage in burdensome work, knead dough for bread, or work in mines. Nevertheless, the repeated insistence on these regulations suggests that they were rarely adhered to. Domestic work was also regulated: women and children were to receive a legally mandated wage and they could not be compelled to work against their will (Ots Capdequi 1976, 102–104). We find women working as spinners, weavers, hat makers, cobblers, and in similar occupations, grouped in guilds where some were master crafters, and as workers in tobacco factories, where they alternated with male workers. They also made handcrafts in the home. Family fabric shops, where cotton was woven, existed before the conquest. During the colonial period, they added wool. Throughout this period, these shops would alternate with *obrajes* to supply textiles. Although the upper classes wore fabrics imported from afar, "throughout nearly the entire colonial era, the cloth of everyday life in Mexico was made by peasant women, families of artisans and crafters in *obrajes*" (Tutino 1985, 35). These activities were common for women in and around Puebla, Tlaxcala, Querétaro, and Mexico City.

Women who belonged to the criollo class received an education, whereas mestizas received instruction that can best be described as charity-run orphanage education. Girls received rudimentary education in the home of an *"amiga"*[10] that had been turned into a school, as mandated by a 1601 Royal Warrant. These schools provided instruction in basic subjects: elementary reading and writing, arithmetic, religion, and, above all, domestic chores, in particular manual ones (embroidery, decorative arrangements, etc.). Girls could also receive an education in convents through the personal instruction of a nun. Schools in the large cities taught elementary subjects. The first public schools opened in 1755.

Women's education varied greatly depending on their social class; however, all schools taught the religious and moral principles that governed women's behavior in every aspect of their lives and that were intended to maintain family traditions. Pilar Gonzalbo (1987b, 128) maintains that, although we can say that women were uneducated, much importance was placed on their education. It was felt that women who oversaw a household, even Spaniards holding the highest status, needed little knowledge; their function was to produce a large number of offspring, and "to fulfill that duty, women do not need . . . 'eloquence or to speak well, great skills of ingenuity, or [the ability to] administrate cities, [or] memory or liberality.' A functioning of hormones, an adequate physical resistance, and a health that would be another of the gifts to transmit, suffice" (Castellanos 1973, 26–27).

In the colonial system, then, education did not guarantee women any social advantage: although illiterate, Sor Juana Inés de la Cruz's mother succeeded in managing her hacienda by using what were clearly her natural talents. And Sor Juana ([1690] 1929, 33–34), an obvious exception to the gender standard for that period, wrote: "Many prefer to leave their daughters barbarous and uncultured, rather than expose them to such a notorious danger as [is] familiarity with men."

Women who aspired to a higher level of knowledge needed financial support to pay a private tutor, as well as the permission of a tolerant father. Naturally, this option was limited to Spanish, criolla, and Indian women belonging to the nobility (Muriel 1982, 497). We need only recall that Sor Juana's concern with attending the university caused her to fantasize about the possibility of disguising herself as a man.

The upper classes were organized into extended families, with several married couples and their children living in a single house (Giraud 1982, 64–65). What today is thought of as the "nuclear family" would not become prevalent until the eighteenth century, although it is clear that regional studies will have to be carried out to determine what variations existed. Women looked after the home, with the help of domestic servants, the number of whom varied according to the economic level, although there were customarily several. Women also took part in church activities and social life. Marriage continued to be considered the most appropriate institution for women, and motherhood was their natural vocation. The social morality that was advocated for women was inspired in the writings of Juan Luis Vives (*Instrucción de la mujer cristiana* [Instruction of the Christian woman]) and Fray Luis de León (*La perfecta casada* [The perfect married woman]). Marriage bonds were defined as unique and indissoluble; hence divorce was merely a physical separation that did not break the vow taken before God. Marriage constituted the only valid option for sexuality, which, within this setting, resembled an obligation (known as a *débito*, or duty), since it was intrinsically tied to reproduction, to the continuity of the family line. Therefore, any expression or preference that excluded procreation, either in action or in thought, was considered a sin. This included homosexuality, masturbation, and even erotic dreams. Virginity, in this context, acquired a superlative value: being single was not the same as being a maiden, and only maidens could guarantee purity and modesty.

Marriages were normally arranged by the parents, and the dowry played a crucial role in the transaction. The personal preference of the contracting parties had little bearing on the decision; nevertheless, young people would resort to various tactics to be united with the mate of their choice, including abduction, secret marriage, or sexual relations in exchange for a promise of marriage, which obliged the family to organize a wedding. A 1776 Royal Decree (Pragmática Real) strengthened parental authority by banning the usual mechanisms by which people managed to marry the person of their choice. This process is the opposite of what took place in Europe, where parental influence over the selection of children's mates tended to decrease (Seed 1988, passim, especially 227).

People married at a young age. In the case of girls, marriage could be agreed upon as early as seven years of age, and they might marry at twelve (Muriel 1974, 19), although the average age for women was around twenty. Among the more affluent classes, the woman provided a dowry, which was administrated by her husband and returned in the event of divorce. The groom furnished "coins," which were worth 10 percent of his patrimony, to guarantee the support of his bride. Wives were entitled to receive the *bienes gananciales*, or community property, that is, 50 percent of what was acquired during the marriage, because domestic work was recognized as necessary. Women were also allowed to receive a special inheritance from their parents, known as "paraphernal" property, which their husband could not touch.

Through marriage women were placed under the authority of their husbands. According to civil law, the wife had to obey her husband and waive her rights regarding most legal actions, properties, and financial gains, and even be subordinate in her domestic activities. The church, although it approved of these principles, was often a woman's ally, since canon law conferred equal rights and obligations on husbands and wives—for example, the consideration that the *débito* should be accepted by both parties, the need for reciprocal assistance and for shared responsibilities vis-à-vis children, and the tenet by which adultery committed by either the husband or the wife was grounds for separation. Nevertheless, separation could be requested only in the event that the transgression had occurred in the couple's home, thereby causing scandal and public shame for the legitimate spouse (Arrom 1985b, 111–112). Regarding the crime of adultery, the law was interpreted more harshly for women than for men. Spanish women and mestizas who violated this law were handed over, along with their lover, to their husband, who could mete out whatever punishment he saw fit—even death—with the proviso that the same punishment be imposed on both parties (Ots Capdequi 1976, 110). Indian adulteresses were treated with greater leniency, apparently because of their status as minors.

In the event of divorce, whether because of adultery, abuse, or contagious disease, women were placed in a house of seclusion (*casa de*

recogimiento). This institution was created in the first half of the
sixteenth century and administered by the church to protect women
with legal problems. The *casas* gradually became a space for voluntary,
temporary spiritual retreat. They took in orphans, single and married
women, and widows, be they Indians, mestizas, or Spaniards. There were
also correctional *casas* that were responsible for guiding women who
had strayed from accepted social norms (Muriel 1974, 518) and that
frequently were filled with prostitutes who were treated as if in prison.
In 1667, Concepcionist nuns were able to rehabilitate the courtesans at
the Recogimiento de Jesús de la Penitencia, and later turned the *casa* into
the Convento de Nuestra Señora de la Balvanera (Muriel 1978, 14). *Casas
de recogimiento* also accepted widows, since the work that was carried
out (manual labor, cooking) in these institutions provided a degree of
safety not always found in the outside world (Muriel 1974, 219). Proper-
tied widows were normally allowed to administrate their businesses or
land, thereby acquiring an enviable independence vis-à-vis society.
Consequently, even some single mothers who hoped to see their children looked after or well-off, independent-minded women pretended to
be widows (Malvido 1990, 126–127).

In the sixteenth and seventeenth centuries, single women apparently
were not rejected, since, according to Christian thinking, the chaste
solitude of nuns was an ideal life. Silvia Arrom (1985b, 110) finds that in
the late eighteenth and early nineteenth centuries there were numerous
single women in Mexico City; she calculates that by 1811 one-third of
women were single, although this does not mean that they did not have
or had not had some type of companion. Patricia Seed (1994, 91–125) has
analyzed the refusal to marry of many young women being courted in the
seventeenth and eighteenth centuries, who preferred to prolong the
courtship period even though their children were considered illegitimate.

The rigid sexual mores of the colonial system brought about a struggle
between body and spirit in which the latter often lost. Rules were
frequently ignored, and extramarital relations occurred in all ethnic
groups (Lavrin 1984, 30–31). Evidence of this is found in the Inquisition
Tribunals, which attest, as well, to the close link between lay and
religious life. Indians were not subject to the guardianship of the Holy
See; hence we are deprived of the possibility of learning of their "deviations." Through the confessional, "perversions" were brought to the
attention of the Tribunal, which dealt with cases of adultery, bigamy,
rape and statutory rape, homosexuality, "simple" fornication (that is,
between unmarried persons), and even the tribulations of priests who
solicited affairs with their parishioners.[11]

The church was generally tolerant: It appears to have established strict rules with the knowledge that the weakness of the flesh would lead to transgressions. The exception was male homosexuality, the "abominable sin." Although we have no knowledge of cases of lesbianism, Serge Gruzinski (1979, 255) maintains that men "were the only ones who paid with death for what was merely the manifestation of their [sexual] uniqueness."

Relations with prostitutes were considered minor deviations, and the practice was even sanctioned by the authorities, who deemed it a necessary evil. As early as 1538, houses of prostitution were authorized, although it is clear that there were also clandestine establishments, as well as prostitutes who worked independently. In 1538, Queen Isabel authorized the construction of a bordello in Mexico City (Atondo 1992, 38). In 1542, the city council chose a building for it, on what was later called "la calle de las Gayas" (street of the merry women; Muriel 1974, 34).[12]

The church's very discourse had opened the door to the arguments that would be used by the accused to defend themselves: dealing with merchants of love was a venial, not a mortal, sin, and its gravity was reduced if a payment was made in exchange for the act and if the offender had been with a given woman only once. Hence, prostitution appears as an accepted complement to marriage; at most, the Crown attempted to offer women alternatives to this practice, since the dearth of well-paid occupations for women and the abundance of candidates (by the eighteenth century there were as many as 3.5 women for each man [Muriel 1974, 37]) caused the ranks of houses of prostitution to swell, no matter how many attempts were made to promote "houses of God" (convents), houses of seclusion, and marriage. We know of charitable works through which young girls with little money were given dowries in order to become nuns or marry, so that they would not further increase the size of the brothels.

Prostitutes were routinely forgiven (because of the intrinsic weakness of their sex?); instead, it was procurers who were punished (Atondo 1982, 280). The latter were marginalized insofar as their activity was considered harmful for modest women. A 1544 testimony indicates that by that time prostitutes had sufficient economic resources to enjoy a place of privilege, which brought about complaints and the subsequent limit on excesses:

> [B]ecause I have been informed that amorous [that is, public] women, when they leave their houses, wear very long and fancy skirts . . . and [take] cushions and rugs to church, as is done by the wives of gentlemen and persons of quality, [giving] a bad example of the Republic because the former *cannot be distin-*

guished from the latter. I order that henceforth these women's skirts may not be held up [by someone else to keep them clean], under penalty of losing the cloak and petticoat they might be wearing, and that they not take a cushion and rug to church, under penalty of losing the cushion and rug, and I order said bailiffs and all authorities to carry this out as such.[13] (Muriel's emphasis)

Sexual deviations were not the only indications of a world that went beyond the strict rules of New Spain. In the early seventeenth century, Bernardo de Balbuena, eager to show *Grandeza mexicana*—"Mexican grandeur," the title of a book he wrote—describes one sector's leisure moments as full of enjoyment, gaiety, and vanity:

> Recreations of pleasures in which to occupy oneself
> of feasts and gifts of a thousand kinds
> to beguile precautions and beguile oneself
>
> conversations, games, tricks, fervors,
> banquets, infinite sweets
> orchards, gardens, hunting, forests, beasts,
>
> pomp, exquisite grandeurs,
> meetings, soirées, pleasant concerts
> music, pastimes and visits;
>
> rejoicements, healthy merriments,
> races, streets, gallantries, strolls,
> friends, in affable taste and treatments

And he continues relating the social tastes that apparently occupied women of great

> beauty and verve
> grace, flair, discretion and cleanliness
> haughtiness, composure and attire. (Balbuena 1974, 68–69)

In his description, Thomas Gage (1982, 179) notes that women, in addition to being lovely, "enjoy so much freedom and like gambling so much that for some among them a day and a night is not enough to finish a first-rate hand [of cards] when they have begun it. And their enthusiasm even [leads them] to publicly invite men to come in their house to gamble." At least, he explains, this is what happened to him. The same author gives us a description of women's wardrobes as being a display of wealth, splendor, luxury and wastefulness—a far cry from the austere image demanded in regulations and sermons. He adds, "Men and women spend extraordinarily on dressing, and their clothes are commonly made of silk[;] . . . precious stones and pearls are . . . in such wide use and they have such vanity in this that there is no more common sight than [that of] diamond cords and clasps in ladies' hats" (1982, 180).

"Ladies" implied those of the upper classes—we would obviously have to add—for whom fashion appears to have required uncomfortable and tight clothing: the portraits show voluminous skirts, overskirts, petticoats, cloaks and mantillas, long sleeves, and high collars that were so stiff they were probably used only on special occasions, among which the most important were portrait days. In the colonial world, attire had a function beyond dress: it was used—more than to cover one's body— to show one's status, race, and class. For this reason, the wardrobe was also regulated, and for this same reason the violation of regulations had a subversive element.

It would seem an exaggeration, then, to imagine the women of New Spain occupied solely in embroidering, carrying out other domestic tasks, and praying. Daily life could be less strict than what some wanted and advocated. In his work on Sor Juana Inés de la Cruz, Octavio Paz recreates a seventeenth century that fluctuated between rigidity and libertinism, pessimism and sensuality, ascetic and erotic sentiments, in which frivolous customs seem to have been accepted without many complications. Paz writes, "The lassitude of the social morality of the Mexican people surely is the legacy of New Spain. We would be ill-advised to denounce it: if *machismo* is a tyranny that darkens the relations between men and women, erotic freedom enlightens them" (1982, 107). The eighteenth century, the "century of depression," appears then as a world in which Isabel Ramírez, Sor Juana Inés de la Cruz's mother, could have children by two different men without marrying either and without bringing either shame or dishonor on herself: clearly there was a close relationship between this mother and her daughters, who were able to marry or enter the convent. The problems faced by Sor Juana arose not because of moral zeal but rather because of a lack of money, since by then being a criolla in and of itself was no longer sufficient to ensure economic security. Her problems also stemmed from being a woman who aspired to the male world of knowledge.

This knowledge, with its requirements of time and freedom, could be attained solely in the convent: the house of God, which was a house different from that of the family but one that also implied an option for a respectable life and thus one to which many women turned. Not all of them were motivated by the desire to know; some sought security, since they lacked the protection of a father or mother; others hoped to avoid marrying outside of their social class or entering houses of prostitution. Because Christian morality idealized chastity, the religious life was the purest and most cherished option a woman could make.

Josefina Muriel (1978, 14) suggests that for women life in the convent was not so different from secular life, since in both cases seclusion and the centrality of devotion in one's activities were the norm.[14] Nevertheless, nuns enjoyed a palpable security. As children, girls learned to value the life of religious women by visiting their aunts or relatives who were in the convent, playing with dolls dressed in religious habits, and delighting in processions or other religious celebrations. Hence, requests to enter the convent were plentiful throughout the colonial period and even in the early nineteenth century. During the viceroyal era there were more than sixty convents of every order and in varying conditions, and hundreds of women made their homes there (ibid., 14).

To become a nun a woman had to spend one year as a novice before being professed during a celebration of much splendor and luxury in which the entire community took part. Streets were lighted and decorated, fireworks were set off, and the candidate wore an opulent dress: this was the day of her wedding with God. Later on, a dowry was paid to the church by her family or her "godfather." In the case of a novice from a poor family, the dowry might be paid by a benefactor. Muriel (ibid., 12) estimates that three thousand pesos was sufficient; with this one-time donation the nun would receive lodging, clothing, and food for the rest of her life. With an additional sum, she could have the services of a maid or even a slave. Only the austere orders denied comfort.

On occasion, convents were founded as payment for a candidate's dowry or by wealthy believers who expected to be rewarded with prayers for their souls (Muriel 1974, 44).

Spaniards, mestizas, and criollas could live in convents. Illegitimacy technically prevented women from being professed, although this impediment could be removed by obtaining a royal warrant (*cédula real*). *Castas* and black women rarely entered the convent as nuns, except as servants. Only rarely were Indian women deemed apt to take vows, until 1724, the year in which the Corpus Christi Franciscan Convent was established for cacique indigenous women. Thereafter, similar houses were founded in Oaxaca and Morelia (Gallagher 1985, 201).

Women in convents enjoyed the company and support of other women, with whom they conversed, read scripture, and prayed while carrying out their tasks. They made beautiful handcrafts (known as "marvels produced by nuns' hands") and culinary delicacies, such as *mole* and chocolate, which required time, skill, and care. Convents also allowed women to educate girls who attended the cloister for training and exposure to high culture. Nevertheless, few nuns knew Latin, which limited their ability to read the great thinkers. Still, some nuns wrote poetry, biographies, plays, or theological treatises, as well as kitchen recipes; others applied themselves in music and painting (Muriel 1982). Not all women who wrote did so for pleasure. In the case of mystics and *iluminati*, their confessors demanded they do so for the church authorities to corroborate their experiences.[15] Muriel (1978, 26) reports that in the least austere orders women were allowed to smoke. Some nuns held positions in the convent as abbesses, secretaries, chroniclers, or accountants, and we can assume that there could have been surreptitious envies, arguments, and problems between them. We know of one such quarrel: in 1701, during a rebellion at the Convento de la Concepción, the nuns wanted to kill the abbess; however, the incident was not made public and the reasons for it are not known (Muriel 1978, 105).

Nuns appear to have led lives with constant activities, including frequent participation in solemn community events. Despite being cloisters, convents had links to the secular world: visits from friends and family, meals offered to high civil and church authorities, religious feasts, professions of new members, among others. Apparently there were convents for every preference; hence Sor Juana was able to choose one where discipline was lax and where she could develop her intellect. In the eighteenth century, there were orders in which vows were not for life and in which assigned duties, such as caring for the sick or praying, were closely related to the outside world (Arrom 1985b, 47–52).

The daily lives of women in New Spain speak of a complex, nuanced universe that included rigors but also pleasures. Here, as with other topics, the answers to our many questions are beginning to emerge.

Sor Juana Inés de la Cruz: A Significant Exception

Sor Juana Inés de la Cruz is an outstanding example of a woman's situation during the period in which she lived, although hers is an exceptional, atypical case. She was endowed with an insatiable intellectual curiosity, leading her to possess a remarkable erudition and to produce an extremely vast oeuvre. In early adolescence, she was part of the retinue of the Countess de Mancera, the wife of the Viceroy of New Spain, who held her in high regard. The viceroyal court of the period was characterized by its gay, worldly, and markedly erotic atmosphere. At the age of twenty-one, Sor Juana entered the San Jerónimo Convent, after having failed to become a member of the Cloistered Carmelites, where discipline was rigid. The San Jerónimo Convent allowed her to exercise her intellectual curiosity, and it boasted one of the best libraries of its time: "I became a religious because, although I knew that the vows had many things (I am speaking of the accessory ones, not the formal ones) that were repugnant to my nature, [given] the total rejection I had of marriage, [this] was the least disproportionate and most decent [option] that I could choose in terms of the security I wished regarding my salvation" ([1690] 1929, 14).

She describes her nature as one of "wanting to live alone . . . not wanting to have an obligatory occupation that would restrict [her] freedom to study, nor the noise of a community that would hinder the placid silence of [her] books" (ibid.). The dowry she needed to enter this situation of privilege in the convent was provided by her mentor, Juan Sentís de Chavarría. Once inside the order, she increased her property by lending money at interest. Clearly her profound love for letters and culture could not have found a better milieu in which to be developed.

Nonetheless, even in the convent she was to face harsh criticism because of her restlessness. Her *Respuesta a Sor Filotea de la Cruz* (Response to Sister Filotea de la Cruz)—an invented character with whom she dialogues during a controversy with the bishop of Puebla— relates certain obstacles that she encountered. Sor Juana, feeling the pressure of an entire system, makes an effort to be more moderate.[16] She was concerned about topics that in her time were not openly discussed, and she clearly ran up against gender limitations: "His Majesty [God] . . . knows that I have asked him to extinguish the light of my understanding, leaving only what is sufficient to abide by his Law, since, according to some, everything else is unnecessary in a woman, and there are even those who say that it is harmful" (ibid., 12).

Nevertheless, she fiercely defended her need to delve into all spheres of knowledge, and she is an example of an education that was solid for her time: she wished to learn something about every field, making her equally curious about letters, sciences and classics, astronomy and physics. In a period governed by obscurantist Spain (the Spain of Charles II, "The Bewitched") and in which New Spain was becoming rapidly institutionalized, gradually closing the escape valves that had left breathing room in society and thus creating contradictions, Sor Juana's knowledge was exhaustive. Although on multiple occasions she was forced to give up her studies, she strenuously defended this predilection. In *Respuesta* she explains the enormous sacrifice this entailed. She recalls, for example, when her superiors had forbidden her to study: "I . . . obeyed regarding not picking up a book[; however,] regarding not studying at all, since this is not within my power, I could not [comply], because, although I did not study books, I studied all the things that God created, hence all of this universal machinery served me as letters and book" (ibid., 126).

She drew conclusions from the line drawn by a spinning top, from the reaction of food when being cooked, and she wrote, "If Aristotle had cooked, he would have written much more" (ibid., 28). Hence, she had an open mind that saw God's word, his Gospel, in all the work created by Him.

At a time when women's education was deemed all but baneful, the Tenth Muse felt that, in accordance with Saint Peter's admonitions, women should be more cultured. In *Respuesta*, she says that she learned to read at the age of three in one of the local schools, or "amigas" schools.

The patriarchal system, more than any other circumstance, was the root cause of the oppression suffered by Sor Juana; in her waning years, it made her abandon her library and studies. Much has been made of her masculine characteristics; however, in her world, the only way to gain access to a universe beyond the walls of a house or convent was by behaving in ways unrelated to gender-specific roles. Undoubtedly, Sor Juana was aggressive, competitive, lucid, ambitious—qualities that contrasted with the submissiveness and docility that were considered "natural" in a woman. The figure of the Tenth Muse reflects a specific oppression, and her open hostility toward the gender-based stratification of her time rightly makes her the precursor of feminist consciousness.

The Bourbons and New Ideas: From Spain to Mexico

In 1700, the dynasty of the Bourbons took over as rulers of Spain, replacing the House of Austria, or Hapsburgs. Their liberal, French-influenced ideas inspired a series of reforms throughout the kingdom that took effect in New Spain beginning in 1765. One important aspect of these reforms was the colonization of the entire territory, which encouraged that of the so-called internal provinces, that is, those of the north: El Pueblo de Nuestra Señora la Reina de Los Angeles, for example, was founded in 1781 by "women, men and children . . . who belonged to the peasant and artisan classes of the northwest of Mexico" (Castillo and Ríos Bustamante 1989, 13). Antonia I. Castañeda (1990) notes that for indigenous women the process of colonization meant systematic sexual abuse.

The second half of the eighteenth century ushered in many changes, especially those that paved the way to capitalist development, with the consequent fostering of private property, thereby altering Spain's oldest corporative tradition. The Bourbons hoped to introduce European progress to the peninsula and its backward colonies, and to that end they issued reforms to regulate the economy and to allow a more equitable distribution of property in New Spain (among the wealthy), stymieing the ascendant "Consulate of Merchants" and clashing with the church. These reforms unwittingly cleared the way for political independence,

and the liberal principles on which they were based would be a fundamental reference point once independence was achieved, especially
among the most forward-looking sectors.

This was an era of splendor: wealth flowed from the mines and
commerce benefited many sectors. We associate these years with excess;
with churrigueresque art forms; with dresses worn by Spanish women
that were even more laden with gold and precious stones, at least in
portraits; with the headdresses worn by nuns on the day they professed
so large that it seems unlikely that they could have held them up alone.
Here we are entering a more open world, which is evident in the
restrictions enacted by the authorities: the Inquisition banned a number
of books that portrayed the world as a place of pleasure, the notion that
happiness could be attained on earth—a place where amusement, adven-
ture, and mischief were possible (Ramos Soriano 1982). Dances were
banned for being blatantly erotic in both the lyrics of the songs and in the
body movements that accompanied the rhythm of the music. Hence, the
chuchumbé, pan de manteca, jarabe gatuno, saranguandingo, and
many others were forbidden but nevertheless systematically danced to,
mostly by the popular classes (Robles Cahero 1985). The social upper
class tended to dance to ballroom music, which was more proper and
reserved. Carnivals also appeared in the eighteenth century (Dallal 1987,
56), and with them, sinful dances flaunted their popularity.

Mixed marriages were more common in the last fifty years of the
colonial period. In 1810, in a collective wedding celebrated in the
Metropolitan Cathedral for 184 couples, one marriage was between a
Spanish man and a black woman, seven were between Spanish men and
Indian women, and at least ten were between Spanish women and Indian
men (Mörner 1974, 99). Mixed marriages were more socially accepted by
this time, although when they involved blacks, they still caused concern
or uneasiness. Mulattos were more easily accepted than were blacks.

As part of this enlightened spirit, an attempt was made to classify into
categories appropriate for analysis the different groups that had emerged
through the two previous centuries. Hence, the classic categories of
gachupín (Spaniard), criollo, mestizo, *negro,* and *mulato* gave way to
chamizo, saltapatrás, lobo, coyote, tente-en-el-aire, albarrasado, and
zambo,[17] among many others. Indians were increasingly marginalized,
both territorially and socially. The heir to this melting pot, in which it
was difficult to distinguish any single race, would own the future. In that
disarray, Mexicanness gradually took shape: race was decreasingly
important, and the fundamental distinction was between subordinates
and possessors. When the independence movement began, the term
indio referred more to a social hierarchy than to a racial one. Neverthe-

less, name and status remained important. Later on, this would be a key element of political independence.

A symbol of these open and chaotic times is the figure of María Ignacia de Valasco y Osario Barba, "La Güera" (light-skinned) Rodríguez—a beautiful, intelligent, ingenious woman, famous for her coquetry and amorous adventures: she had three husbands and, apparently, several lovers, including, according to tradition, Simón Bolívar, Alexander von Humboldt, and Agustín de Iturbide. Her first husband, the Marqués de Villamil, accused her before the Divorce Tribunal of repeated adultery; she, in turn, accused him of frequent physical abuse (Arrom 1976, 63–108), which was a common practice among husbands in those years. An important part of the myth represented by "La Güera" is her support for Mexico's independence. Her image expresses the limits and possibilities for a woman of talent in this period of change and continuity.

In a study that traces the role of women through four generations of the family of the counts of Regla, from 1750 to 1830, Edith Couturier (1978, 129–149) maintains that women participated in public life more than had been believed, in the shadow of the family, but from a position of authority. This was a wealthy family that was both a kinship network and a business network in which married and single women had a role. Although this study of a particular family allows the author to generalize about women's participation in colonial Mexico, it is important to note that the family in question belonged to the aristocracy and that other classes have not yet been sufficiently examined.

Among the working classes, women continued to ply their wares in the street, perform public services, and work as maids. We also find them at the center of artisan families. As a sector, artisans suffered frequent crises. In 1789, for example, following a free-trade decree, the market was flooded with Catalonian fabrics (Tutino 1985, 40). When such crises occurred, the owners of *obrajes* could declare that they "found it more advantageous to have all their wool woven by women from the poorest rural families" (ibid., 38). Hence, these women's share of the domestic workload increased. The artisan sector was vulnerable and was apparently strongly affected by Mexico's independence. In a testimony given around 1829, Doña Clara Verdad ("Clear Truth") and Doña Juana Valiente ("Joan Valiant") were conversing and lamenting the illness of a third woman, Doña Crecencia, during a period of decline in the artisan sector. The women comment on their misfortune: "This poor family was still supported in decent [conditions] in the year twenty, according to my count: it supported six weavers who worked with silk; six or eight winders; two spooling girls; one [worker] who would warp *rebozos*: . . . More than twenty were supported by making these trinkets, [allowing]

Crecencia's family to breathe comfortably; but then foreign ribbons began to enter" the country (Chávez 1977, 42–43).

Women were also employed in tobacco factories, which during the last fifty years of the colonial period were the second most important industry, after mining, employing 43.3 percent of women workers, especially in temporary and piecework, in which they had to carry out more tasks and they received lower wages (Ros 1985 62–63).

The church was also affected by the reforms. It was common for nuns to rent out houses in the city and for convents to function as credit institutions; since there were no banks, the church acted as a money-lender. In 1769, steps had been taken to curb the ostentation of wealth in the convents and to limit the gifts that nuns could receive as well as the number of servants they could have; nevertheless, they refused to abide by these restrictions (Lavrin 1965). Between 1804 and 1809, the Bourbons, who were at war with England and in need of money, implemented a system of *reales cédulas,* or royal warrants,[18] by which landowners who had received mortgages from the church or who otherwise owed it money, and the church itself, were obliged to sell their property to contribute to the Royal Fund. This episode affected the clergy and its protégés, among whom resistance or refusal to forfeit benefits was common.

The eighteenth century ushered in greater civil equality—a requirement for the development of capital. To a large degree the touchstone was education; hence the idea that both sexes should benefit from it was fomented. This change was seen clearly in Europe. The marquis de Condorcet, a French philosopher, had asked that women be given the right to vote, to receive an education, and to work.[19] In 1792 in England, Mary Wollstonecraft had written a declaration in favor of the women's cause: *Vindication of the Rights of Woman* focused on education, among other rights. In Spain, Benito Feijóo offered guidelines regarding social sexual morality. In "Defensa de las mujeres" (Defense of women), he rejects the idea of women's inferiority, although he does maintain that men have greater aptitude for civic life. The purpose of educating women was, then, to ensure that they better fulfill the sexual role assigned to them within the home, allowing them to contribute to the development of the system. Consequently, although there was theoretical discourse supporting a change in attitudes, in practice, education does not appear to have changed much.

In 1767, the San Ignacio Girls School, also known as the "Vizcaínas," was founded. Although it was run by lay persons, it did not change either traditional methodology or content. By the late eighteenth century it was felt that teaching should conform to social differences: "Humility, poverty, obedience, patience in suffering, tolerance of injuries, resignation and an unyielding faith in eternal life was what poor women, women workers, needed, as a stereotype of what traditional education had been. Grace and self-assurance, knowledge of fashion, agility and rhythm in dance, pleasantness in conversation and musical ability were the elements of a good education for young aristocratic women" (Gonzalbo 1985, 115–116).

At the dawn of independence the ideas inspired by Feijóo were still in vogue. In 1819, José Joaquín Fernández de Lizardi published *La Quijotita y su prima* (The little Quijote girl and her cousin), in which he juxtaposes two forms of women's education: traditional education as received by Pomposita, which resorts to the lash, the cane, and pricks or needles to aid with the memorization of Father Ripalda's 1591 catechism—the most widely accepted code of conduct, which would continue to be used until the twentieth century—contrasted with innovative, modern education, which he deemed the best and which was given to young Prudencia. Although the techniques of the latter type of education were gentler and its pace was slower, the model of women it hoped to shape was quite similar to that of traditional education. The principle was that "[b]y natural law, by divine and civil [law], woman, generally speaking, is always inferior to man" (quoted in Gonzalbo 1985, 135).

Nevertheless, motherhood was believed to make women the "first and main actresses in the propagation of human lineage" (ibid.), from whence social division stems: "[M]ay it remain for women to be the enjoyment, the rest, the greatest honest pleasure of men, the repository of their trust, the balm of their troubles, the magnet of their affections, the tranquillity of their spirit, the prize of their endeavors, the object of their hopes and the ultimate solace from their adversities and disgraces; may it remain for them, finally, to be the delight of men, the charm of sages, the pleasure of warriors, the throne of kings, the refuge of the just, the first altar of the saints, since all of this will be the mother on whose breasts and in whose arms shall be raised the sages, the kings, the righteous and the saints" (ibid.).

It is clear that motherhood made women depend on men and excluded them from the sphere of public activities, business, politics, and even the cloister, given the latter's chastity requirement. This thinking would prevail for a long time and adapt to diverse circumstances. In 1823, after Mexico had gained independence, a teacher named Ana Josefa Caballero de la Borda, in the inaugural address of a boarding school for girls, pointed to the need to better educate women in order for them, in their role as wives and mothers, to carry forward the projects for the new country. Otherwise, she asked, "What children could they give our society?"[20] She said that her intention was to change the norms that—according to her—made women desirous of luxury, filled them with vanity, pride, and false values, and converted them into an object that their husband did not see as "a companion, but [as] a beautiful statue with which to take pleasure!" (Gonzalbo 1985, 151).

The need for a change that would make the female half of society conform to the new nation's requirements was explicit: women had to be the worthy wives of the new Mexican man. Their own role as persons or citizens continued to be overlooked by the dominant system. Something similar occurred with working women: they had a greater role in production, but they could hardly consider their work an element of liberation. Their specific oppression was no longer based on race as much as on class and sex, and it took place within a context of open conflicts, the circulation of political ideas, and circumstances that were favorable for the country's emancipation, for the transition from New Spain to Mexico. In this setting, to what degree would Mexican women be able to emancipate themselves?

3

Mexican Women in the Nineteenth Century
Idols of Bronze or
Inspiration of the Home?

ༀ ༀ

Mexico as a nation was born in 1821 with the success of the independence movement, which was closely linked to the Bourbonic reforms
aimed at economic modernization. This modernization, in turn, was
considered a necessary condition for the country to benefit more from its
ties with European capitalism.

The nineteenth century was politically tumultuous for the new
nation, with frequent wars, riots, and coups d'état. Skirmishes, first
between York Rite and Scottish Rite Freemasons,[1] and later between
federalists and centralists, marked the early part of the century and led
to battles between Liberals and Conservatives, culminating in the Three
Years' War (1858–1861).

Against this backdrop, Texas seceded from Mexico in 1836 and was
annexed by the United States in 1845, bringing Mexico to war with its
northern neighbor. Following the war, and pursuant to the 1848
Guadalupe-Hidalgo Treaty, Mexico lost the territories of New California and New Mexico and forfeited Texas in exchange for fifteen million
pesos. In the process, the country relinquished more than half its
territory: 925,000 square miles.

The 1861 French intervention, carried out by Napoleon III at the
request of a group of Mexican Conservatives, imposed the Second
Empire on the country under the rule of a European prince, Maximilian
of Hapsburg, who arrived with his wife, Carlota, in 1864 and remained
until 1867, when he was executed by the Liberals.

The nineteenth century saw an attempt to put liberal ideals into
practice. These ideals included private property, free enterprise, and the
dismantling of the "corporations," of which the clearest examples were
the Catholic Church and the community of Indian peoples. During the
entire nineteenth century, one sector—the Liberals—that had first
emerged during the colonial period, promoted this national program.
During this critical period, the members of this sector confronted those
who hoped to preserve the social and economic structure of New Spain

for their own benefit. Hence, each side defended a national ideal that reflected not only their interpretation of the present and past but their plans for the future as well. Whereas Conservatives attempted, as their name indicates, to maintain long-established structures, Liberals hoped to erase the past and bring about a new present that would give Mexico a different position within the "family of nations."

The nineteenth century's constant political and military turmoil became increasingly radicalized; hence, problems were continual. The state was weak and local powers were strong; banditry and contraband were widespread; the economy and population grew at a painfully slow pace; the financial system was precarious (the first bank was not established until 1864). Mexicans saw their private world, the home, as the source of order and stability. Despite their different political positions, the various factions clearly agreed in their ideas concerning women.

The 1857 Constitution and the 1859 Reform Laws represented the triumph of Liberal ideology, providing the country with a legal framework for the development of capitalism and the emergence of a bourgeoisie. The new constitution theoretically guaranteed equality of all persons; nevertheless, the great social and economic disparities made this ideal impossible to carry out. Inequality of the sexes was especially pronounced. Laws, in and of themselves, were perceived as agents of change: it was believed that appropriate legislation would generate conditions that had not been brought about by social dynamics alone.

In 1867, in the wake of successive civil wars, changes of government, two empires, and various foreign interventions, the monarchists were definitively defeated and republican rule was restored. The Restored Republic meant peace and the opportunity to implement the ideals that constant warfare had forestalled. Benito Juárez, a full-blooded Zapotec Indian, rose—through what was clearly an enormous effort—from child sheep herder to president of the Republic. He married Margarita Maza, the criolla daughter of his former employers. Together, Juárez and Maza exemplify the attempt to surpass racial status and to succeed on the basis of prestige, ideas, and money.

With the Restored Republic, guided first by Juárez and later by Porfirio Díaz, the nation embarked on an openly capitalist path. The three decades of *porfirismo*, in particular, ushered in economic growth, driven by ideals that called for "order and progress" and "few politics and much administration." The nineteenth century can be seen as a period in which laws were promulgated and people believed in them,[2] although it is clear that in practice the body of laws inherited from New Spain remained, to a large degree, in effect. Indeed, until the 1870 Civil Code was issued, each ethnic group was governed in accordance with its own norms. Racial distinctions were banned in 1822, as were titles of nobility in 1829 and artisans' guilds in 1856.

All aspects of life became increasingly secularized. The Reform Laws were not the only encumbrance on the church's political and economic power; clerics had less influence on values, and this affected women. The 1857 Civil Registry Law led to the establishment of civil marriage in 1859, according to which only children whose parents had been married in a civil ceremony were legitimate. Despite his status as a foreign emperor, Maximilian also had liberal ideas, and he promulgated the Civil Registry Law of 1865.

Throughout the nineteenth century—so tumultuous and filled with political projects—there were elements of continuity. Mentality and sentiments change gradually and at their own pace; they pervade daily life and give values to society, despite political changes, and link the colonial period to the nation-state through what people think, believe, eat, and say; they are the invisible thread common to different classes that may confront political or social similarities in culture, language, religion, and customs. Reality is shaped through objects, attitudes, and values, and is freely re-created on a private level. Hence, when we ask ourselves about women—women who belong to different social classes and political parties—our questions go beyond ideas, although these ideas rest on an ineffable structure. We are dealing with a social morality constructed over several centuries and based on rigid archetypes, but we are also dealing with the variants in accepted morality and the options for gradually surpassing imposed traditions.

The common domain for nineteenth-century Mexican women was the home: among Yorks and Scots, federalists and centralists, Liberals and Conservatives, women devoted their efforts to maintaining peace and order in the private sphere, to keeping the world of reproduction safe. Women bore children, and they continued to be exemplary mothers of soldiers who died in battle, of laborers who worked in the first factories, of peasants who toiled in the fields, and of the leaders and caudillos of an era marked by constant warfare. Their role was precisely defined: to maintain the place where the warrior could rest from warfare, whether military or industrial or entrepreneurial. They were essential for the reproduction of soldiers and laborers.

Work in the home was still recognized and valued. Thus, women needed to educate themselves to do their tasks as well as possible. Values that were deemed eternal in women were readapted to the specific needs of the moment. The different expressions of romanticism exalted virtues considered basic to women's nature: delicateness, moral superiority, and spirituality. However, women remained at home, only now adorned as muses.

When it was felt necessary for them to do so, they entered the factory: since their labor was required, the percentage of women employed in production rose. Peasant women also continued to work in the age-old tasks required by rural life, and in the cities women worked as tortilla makers, *atole* makers, and seamstresses. Rarely did women participate in political or military struggles. When they did take part, their role stood out because of their spirit of sacrifice or because of their surprising heroic actions, rather than because of the tenacious conduct that inevitably would have required another system of feminine values. The model woman continued to be docile and submissive, centered in her home, and focused on her children. In addition to the double workday, women workers had to endure the tacit or open accusation that they were abandoning their "natural" condition.

The artisan class became increasingly fragmented. The convent continued to be an option, although it was resorted to less and less. Between 1828 and 1850, Spanish women who chose religious life in Mexico City decreased from 2.8 percent to 1.3 percent (Arrom 1985b, 142–144). This challenges the claim that women's only alternatives were marriage or the convent. Between 1790 and 1850 the number of cloistered nuns in Mexico City decreased by nearly 40 percent, stabilizing at 540 and remaining there until convents were closed in 1863 (ibid., 48). In 1861 the number of convents in Mexico City declined from 22 to 9 (ibid., 48).

Women's negligible political participation does not imply a clear-cut separation between public and private affairs, since the interaction between these two spheres was fluid. In addition, there were exceptions, and many heroines emerged during the process that unfolded in these years. During the independence movement, Josefa Ortiz de Domínguez and Leona Vicario stand out. The former, the wife of the *corregidor* (mayor) of Querétaro, supported the insurgent troops, and the latter fought in the struggle.

Other women active in the struggle for independence remained anonymous or were little known. In 1821, Josefina Guelberdi expressed her disagreement with women's exclusion from politics.[3] Women opposed the foreign (U.S. and French) interventions by defending their homes and land. Some took part in the resistance as couriers, nurses, spies, etc.; others performed heroic actions, firing canons and fighting in battles. Some took advantage of favorable circumstances, such as Martha Hernández, who was arrested for selling poisoned candy to American soldiers in 1847 (INAH 1985).

Ignacia Riesch disguised herself as a man and fought as a lancer against Maximilian's imperial army. She even became an official, although her valor was not always acknowledged by her subordinates. According to tradition, one day a soldier under her command refused to obey her because she was a woman, and she committed suicide. To participate in public life women often had to be mannish, and frequently not even this was sufficient.[4]

Women who were active on any of the losing sides throughout the century have, naturally, been erased from historiography on two accounts: first, because of their sex, and second, because of the Manichaeism that conditions the findings of a certain historiography to a particular project—that of the group that prevailed and continues to hold power—and to a particular power machinery.

Studying women of that period leads to an obvious temptation: the desire to know more about those heroines, to understand them, to see them as representatives of a social group. The latter would be a false interpretation, however. Although these women experienced common situations, they were the exception, and their roles, however important, were those of extras. The domain of everyday women continued to be the home; their time was devoted to daily routine—regardless of plans, manifestoes, or battles. Generally they were sheltered in the home, where they expressed few opinions and deviated as little as possible from familial ideology. The gender's social archetypes continue to be based on submission.

This is a century of manuals of etiquette, since the numerous changes in public life led to a distrust of usages and customs that had been considered normal. Hence, the printed word of those years was devoted, for the most part, to indicating what woman "should do." Manual Payno and Francisco Zarco, important writers during this period, were experts in the art of giving advice to women, which they published in newspapers and magazines that exalted the role of "keepers of the home."[5]

Participation in politics was incompatible with the role of housewives. Nevertheless, the constant conflicts that jolted the country also affected women's lives. Many years after the political passions had cooled and after the sorrow over lives lost in those convulsive times had supposedly been overcome, Fanny Chambers , an insightful American traveler who became familiar with turn-of-the-century Mexico, pointed out that the melancholy characteristic of Mexicans was stronger in women than in men and that they cried uncontrollably in recalling the persons who had been lost in battle. "They are all patriotic, and if the country suffers, it is a part of themselves, and is reflected in their lives" (Gooch 1887, 200). They suffered in private, in their homes, and their lives normally excluded travel. Gooch adds, "Women, in the seclusion of their homes, have kept an ever-faithful watch over the domestic virtues, and the happiness and welfare of those whom God has given them" (ibid., 199–200), which shows they clearly played the role of guardians of the dominant ideology.

The history of nineteenth-century women has been little studied. Mexican historiography, replete with bronze heroes, has also produced a few female idols, but they come across as cold statues and their stories tell us little about the warm universe of the women who lived amid cooking and embroidery, prayers, chores, and board games. Novels crack the door a bit further. For example, in *Astucia: El jefe de los hermanos de la Hoja o los charros contrabandistas de la Rama* (Astucia: The head of the De la Hoja brothers or of the De la Rama rural smugglers), Luis G. Inclán (1969) conveys feminine characters, anecdotes, histories. It narrates the adventures of, among others, the de la Hoja brothers and the de la Rama horse-riding smugglers, whose frequent adventures stem from their clandestine tobacco trade. Inclán uses these characters to show the customs and social morality of his time, and he portrays the typical upbringing of the well-off rural classes. Camila is the example of a white woman of a lower-class background. She jokes, works, rides horseback, takes initiatives, and looks after her house; keeps warm with a rebozo and braids her hair; suffers because she is an orphan, because she lacks the support of a father and because she is "freeloading" off her sister. She is happy, therefore, to be acceptable to her beloved's father and to marry. She helps us understand some of the traits of nineteenth-century Mexican women. There are other, equally rich, novels. In addition to *Astucia, Clemencia* (Altamirano 1966), *La calandria* (The carriage; Altamirano 1970), and *Los parientes ricos* (The rich relations; Delgado 1961) also portray the family as the only appropriate station for women, and the absence of the father as a cause of women's fragility, leaving them defenseless against the difficulties they encounter. Marriage is presented as the ideal institution for women.

Daily Life and Social Morality

The religious paradigm for women continued to be Mary. Nevertheless, as noted above, in New Spain the ideal of the nun's chaste solitude gradually lost relevance. Still, the Marian ideal established guidelines for women's lives from childhood through courtship, marriage, motherhood, and grandmotherhood. Motherhood was considered the natural life for all women, although its unceasing regulation questions the extent to which it was truly natural. Clearly not all women could fulfill the expectations of the dominant ideology: by 1811 one-third of women in Mexico City were single, and from 1830 to 1842 between 18 percent and 33 percent of children born in the capital were illegitimate (Arrom 1985b, 122–123).

Over the first half of the century, some attitudes toward women in Mexico City changed. In some cases, this entailed an improvement in their legal status, such as the reduction in the age of legal adulthood from twenty-five to twenty-one, and removing single adults from their parents' guardianship. Some measures were proposed to give women social advantages, such as the automatic right of widows and single mothers to custody over their children, the possibility to adopt children and be guardians, parents' authority regarding their children's education, the revocation of a man's right to kill an adulterous wife, the limit on a husband's rights vis-à-vis his spouse's property, and greater rights for single women. All these proposals reflected an increased respect for women's capacity and made several issues public, even if the debates were not always resolved in women's favor. The measures reflected a higher opinion regarding women as well as their own increased self-esteem (ibid., passim, especially 93–97). These matters require further study at the regional level.

As noted, travel testimonies describing the American world, which ranged from the enthusiastic to the disenchanted, provide valuable data. Such is the case, among others mentioned here, of the marquise Calderón de la Barca, the Scottish wife of Spain's first ambassador to Mexico, who lived in the country from 1839 to 1842. Her critical eye perceived details that Mexicans overlooked. Although she often judges too quickly and succumbs to folklorist characterizations, the marquise's perspective is interesting, especially her descriptions of the upper classes of the period. With her obvious intelligence, she realizes, "indeed, it is long before a stranger even suspects the state of morals in this country, for, whatever be the private conduct of individuals, the most perfect decorum prevails in the outward behavior" (Calderón 1970, 290). She makes the questionable observation that gossiping did not exist and notes that liaisons between close friends are viewed with indifference. Years later, Gooch (1887, 230) would confirm this: "I have been told that the women are much given to gossip; but if true, I have not heard them." Calderón adds that "[a]s long as a woman attends church regularly, is a patron of charitable institutions, and gives no scandal in her outward behavior, she can well do pretty much whatever she pleases. As for flirtations in public, they are unknown" (1970, 290). This author, then, conveys a constant that had stood out in the viceroyal period: a divorce between the morality that was required and displayed in public and the morality that was practiced in private life.

Women appear to have vacillated between what was expected of them and what was tolerated; some conflicts women faced, as well as the few options they were able to take advantage of, probably emerged from the ambiguous space outside prescribed norms.

Silvia Arrom (1985b, 13) suggests a continuity in both the procedures and the causes for church-sanctioned divorce between 1850 and 1857, and among the latter was included violence at the hands of men. Violence continued after Mexico's independence, despite the political changes, and it affected all social classes, constituting, therefore, a specific form of gender oppression. Vicente Calvo (1843) observes that among the Indians of Sonora, "women serve their husbands, who reward them with beatings, bludgeonings, kicks, and sorrows." In the first half of the century, this treatment kept alive the colonial institution of the houses of seclusion, where women who had filed for divorce were "deposited" to protect them from spousal excess or abuse. After independence, houses of seclusion were transformed and included among the so-called "houses of welfare and correction" (Muriel 1974, 224). As noted, however, following the passage of the Reform Laws, these institutions lost their financial backing and disappeared. During this period, divorce implied a civil and physical separation that was approved by the church, but that did not break the eternal bond that had been made before God. Although civil marriage was established in 1859, well into the twentieth century religious union continued to be the rule among the popular classes. Between 1800 and 1857 there were some fifteen divorces per year, 92 percent of which had been requested by women who were tired of being mistreated and who dared risk scandal and solitude, even though 40 percent of these women did not know how to write (Arrom 1985b, 14). Women also divorced for reasons that were less and less serious (Arrom 1976, 28; 1985b, 254). Importantly, the authorities were interested in preserving marriage and, therefore, the family, as reaffirmed in the "epistle" (official instruction read at civil marriage ceremonies) drafted by Melchor Ocampo.[6] This document states that "marriage is the only moral means for founding a family, for preserving the species and for overcoming the individual's imperfections." Within it, sexual roles are precisely delimited:

> The man, whose sexual attributes are principally valor and strength, must give, and shall give, protection, food and direction to the woman, treating her always as the party more delicate, sensitive and refined than himself, and with the magnanimity and benevolence that the strong must give to the weak, essentially when this weak one gives herself to him, and when through society she has been entrusted to him. . . . The woman, whose principal attributes are abnegation, beauty, compassion, insight and tenderness, must give and shall give her husband obedience, pleasantness, assistance, solace and advice, treating him always with the veneration that is to be given to the person who supports and defends us, and with the delicateness of

someone who does not wish to irritate the brusque, irritable and hard part of oneself. (Article 15 of the Civil Marriage Law, 1959)

Despite this advice, violence against women in the home also caused them to rebel when they were unable to obtain a divorce and, in extreme cases, to murder their husband.

Calderón de la Barca visited the women's prison and wrote, "It is painful and almost startling to see the first ladies in Mexico familiarly conversing with and embracing women who have been guilty of the most atrocious crimes—especially of murdering their husbands, which is the chief crime of the female prisoners" (1970, 532). Prisoners included women from different social classes, even one woman who had murdered the governor of Mexico—her husband. Their conditions in prison differed depending on their social class. Whereas the rich took classes in reading and Christian doctrine, poor prisoners had to prepare the inmates' meals while their children played amid misery and filth, and where—Calderón de la Barca tells us—"the sense of smell is a doubtful blessing" (ibid., 533). The marquise relates that "[f]ew looked sad, none seemed ashamed . . . it is some comfort to hear that their husbands were generally such brutes that they deserved little better" (ibid.).

Calderón de la Barca portrays upper-class Mexican women as rather frivolous: "Generally speaking, then, Mexican señoras and señoritas write, read and play a little, sew, and take care of their houses and children. When I say they read, I mean that they know how to read; when I say that they write, I do not mean that they can always spell; and when I say they play, I do not assert that they have generally a knowledge of music. . . . In fact, if we compare the education of women in Mexico with that of girls in England or the United States, we should be inclined to dismiss the subject as nonexistent. It is not a comparison, but a contrast" (ibid., 286–287).

Paula Kolonitz, a traveler who came to Mexico with Carlota of Hapsburg's retinue in 1864, says, similarly, "I never saw Mexican ladies with a book in their hands, unless it was the prayer book, nor did I ever see them occupied in any work. If they write, their handwriting shows clearly that they are unaccustomed to doing so; their ignorance is complete and they have no idea what history and geography are. For them, Europe is Spain, from whence their origin comes; Rome, where the Pope rules; and Paris, from whence their dresses arrive" (1984, 107). Calderón (1970, 287) tries to explain this by looking beyond social conditions. For her, "the climate inclines everyone to indolence, both in physical aspects and in morality. . . . I am convinced that it is impossible to take the same exercise with the mind or with the body in this country as in Europe or the northern states." Nevertheless, she also sees coherence between these characteristics and the needs created by the time and situation, that is, the manner in which these women could fulfill specific social requirements. Hence she describes a clear introjection of the socially assigned roles, in which women function precisely as social moderators:

> But if a Mexican girl is ignorant she rarely shows it. They have generally *de grandes dispositions* for music and other accomplishments—and the greatest possible tact, never by any chance wandering out of their depth or by word or look betraying their ignorance or that they are not well informed on the subject under discussion.
>
> The Mexican women are never graceful, yet they are rarely awkward, and always self-possessed . . . they have plenty of natural talent, and where it has been thoroughly cultivated, no women can surpass them. (1970, 288)

This makes Mexican women prized wives for foreigners. The marquise is surprised not so much by their different behavior, such as smoking in public, including large cigars—a fad that Kolonitz (1984, 113) states had passed by the time she made her trip—as by their cultural limitation.

A gray area clearly existed between what women "should do" and their actual conduct, an area that allowed for a double standard, which, in turn, left room for prostitution. If "decent" women had explicit duties that were transmitted through education and that were not compatible with the expression of their sexuality, prostitutes turned this need into a business and were tolerated as a necessary evil. The mechanism was twofold: the sexual freedom of one group of women was taken away and placed in another group, which responded to mercantile criteria; hence the two groups neutralized one another. This distribution of personal capacities caused, on the one hand, shamed women who feared the possibility of pleasure and who justified their actions by their duty to procreate, and, on the other, women who alienated this capacity in commerce. Although this system was not explicit, and even though it may not have been consciously planned, its effect was to deny women's sexuality in order to protect the system of male privilege.

Prostitution was widespread and it was practiced in deplorable conditions. Venereal disease decimated these women, many of whom were barely more than children. For the sake of public health, the church cooperated through the care provided by the Sisters of Charity at the San Juan de Dios Hospital; still, many prostitutes clearly were beyond the reach of health controls. The same nuns also looked after abandoned children, many of whom were probably the sons and daughters of prostitutes. Calderón de la Barca explains the functioning of the *cuna* ("cradle," or "nursery")—an institution that sought indigenous wet nurses for these children (1970, 531). Following the Reforma and the subsequent reduction of the church's social role, these institutions, along with the convents and houses of seclusion, were most likely restricted or eliminated altogether.

During the Second Empire, to protect French soldiers from venereal disease, prostitution began to be regulated through checkups, health monitoring, and photographic records of women who plied this trade. Their images were among the first to be reproduced by a camera.

Women with licentious lifestyles, not all of whom were prostitutes, wore a distinctive style of clothing: the *china poblana* dress that today is part of the nation's folklore. *Chinas* would wear glittery fabrics and bright colors and, most notably, a full, print overskirt. The marquise Calderón de la Barca found this style appealing and considered donning one for a costume ball but was dissuaded, lest doubts be raised regarding her status as a "lady" (1970, 124–125). Clearly, dress was no longer subject to legal regulations, and the access to more disposable income allowed greater adornment and a closer imitation of European fashion. Custom gave dress its significance.

Calvo (1843) relates that "on feast days, merchants of pleasure normally converge at the markets, [and] at the same time they sell essences and perfumes, articles in great demand; gallants come on those days to the market and purchase flowers and perfumes for their mistresses." In numerous engravings of this era, the *chinas* appear surrounded by men looking at them slyly.

Marcos Arróniz (1991, 138) notes that "there is not a street where you cannot see [a *china*], graceful and *galante*, twirling her petticoat from one side of the street to the other; and in the *jarabe*, a dance that is as boisterous as it is national, she captivates with her lascivious movements, with the gaze of her brown or dark eyes."

Women enjoyed taking strolls, going to parties and dances, and visiting friends. Calderón de la Barca (1970, 271) describes their pastimes. Given their delicateness, members of the fair sex took part in activities that in the old world would have been inconceivable, such as games of chance, bullfights, and cockfights, where "even the ladies entered in the spirit of the scene, taking bets with the gentlemen *sotto voce* in their boxes upon such and such favourite animal. . . . It has a curious effect to European eyes to see young ladies of good family, looking in everything else peculiarly feminine and gentle, sanctioning by their presence this savage diversion."

Leisure was also related to social class. Women of lineage would stroll in the Alameda, whereas poor women would do so along the Santa Anita canal; by the mid–nineteenth century, however, this changed; the fiestas held in San Agustín de las Cuevas (now known as Tlalpan), or the celebrations during Carnival, had become distractions for common people, and wealthy women no longer delighted in these celebrations.

Dances and the opera were common pastimes. Being a foreigner, Calderón is surprised by the manner in which upper-class woman liked to adorn themselves, achieving "a monotony of diamond earrings" (ibid., 131). "Their gowns have all a *hunchy* loaded look, all velvet or satin" (ibid., 133). What most caught her eye regarding women's flirtatiousness was that "their feet, naturally small, are squeezed nearly double, Chinese fashion, into little ill-made shoes still smaller—so that they look in front like little horses' hoofs. Of course they can neither dance nor walk" (ibid.). Fashion seemed designed to oppress, with corsets, crinolines, and bustles. To enjoy themselves women had to adhere faithfully to European fashion, often with homemade garments. When doing household chores during the day, they wore comfortable clothes, no corset, and low shoes (Gooch 1887, 237).

By the 1860s, the mantilla was seldom worn, and only the popular classes continued to don the rebozo (Ortega 1853, 37).[7] Each social class had its own fashion. Some indigenous women, however, had preserved and continued to wear the distinctive clothing of their group—pre-Hispanic in origin but regulated during the colonial period. Even today some Indian women can be seen to wear such attire.

Regarding physical appearance, the marquise Calderón de la Barca was not very complimentary toward upper-class women; by contrast, she considered mestizas members of "the handsomest race in Mexico" (1970, 444). She added that *"rancheritas . . .* preserved [their figures] by the constant exercise that country women must per force take, whatever their natural indolence; while the early fading of beauty in the higher classes, the decay of teeth and the overcorpulence so common amongst them, are no doubt the natural consequences of want of exercise and of injudicious food [which included eating meat three times per day and abusing sweets] added perhaps to the effects of climate" (ibid., 155–156). Kolonitz (1984, 110) notes that "the flower of youth is short-lived in the Mexican woman and in maturity she frequently becomes too fat; at times a dark fuzz appears above her upper lip and more than one lady appears very satisfied with her mustache."

Calderón de la Barca finds Indian women ravishingly beautiful. The rural women she describes are extremely attractive and clean, "with the most beautiful teeth imaginable laughing and talking in their native tongue at a great rate as they [are] washing in the brooks—some their hair and others their clothes" (1970, 444); but those who live and work in the city are careless and indolent, and wear "their black hair plaited with a dirty red ribbon, a piece of woolen cloth wrapped round them, and a little mahogany baby hanging behind, its face upturned to the sky and its head jerking along somehow without its neck being dislocated" (ibid., 22). She says their "love for their children amounts to passion" (ibid., 532). She seems to share the common tendency in Mexico at that time of dividing the indigenous race into two groups: Indians who remain marginalized and pure and those who attempt to integrate into society and in the process adopt every vice. Frequently this differentiation was made between Indians of the past and Indians of the present. Kolonitz shares the opinion regarding the unattractiveness and filthiness of indigenous women in the cities, although she states that "they all have an expression of sweetness and of long-suffering resignation" (1984, 117).

Calderón de la Barca comes across as particularly harsh toward maids, whom she describes as lazy women who hide their filthiness under their rebozo and steal at the slightest opportunity. Her obvious inability to understand them stems both from her class position and from her status as a foreigner.

Class determined many aspects of women's lives. Childbirth, for example, was different for indigenous and poor women compared to upper-class women. The former could give birth and continue to grind their corn, whereas the latter gave birth at home assisted by midwives and relatives. Nevertheless, the different classes had some common customs. If, regarding diet, "[b]oth the poor and the rich have a great predilection for tortillas and beans" (ibid., 106), they also shared gender-related similarities in their vanity, for example, the attention they gave to their hair, "that glory of [the Mexican] woman" (Gooch 1887, 230). The manner in which Indian women washed their hair in rivers impressed Calderón de la Barca, and Kolonitz described their hair as blankets that nearly reached their feet (1984, 105).

Women's Work and Family Life

In the early years of Mexican independence, women of the popular classes worked in the fields, in urban services, or as maids. Flora Salazar (1987, table 4) estimates that they were employed as follows: 65.4 percent as servants, 21.18 percent in artisanal industries or in commerce (tobacconists, workers in tobacco factories, seamstresses, spinners, weavers), and 10.03 percent in food services (making *atole*, working in food warehouses or in mills, making tortillas), and the rest in various other activities. Their employment in *obrajes* had been encouraged by an entrepreneur named Esteban de Antuñano in 1837, through a book titled *Ventajas políticas, fabriles y domésticas para dar ocupación también a las mujeres en las fábricas de maquinaria moderna que se están levantando en México* (Political, factory, and domestic advantages for also giving employment to women in the modern-machinery factories that are being constructed in Mexico).

Women of lineage attended to their home, and, according to the marquise Calderón, they did so with great determination; they also taught classes in reading and in Christian doctrine. "With the time which they devote to these charitable offices, together with their numerous devotional exercises, and the care that their houses [and families] require, it cannot be said that the life of a Mexican señora is an idle one nor, in such cases can it be considered a useless one" (1970, 533). Nevertheless, the value accorded to housework gradually disappeared over the course of the century.

Hence, wealthy women ruled over their private domains, which they attended to with much care. Politeness in a woman was essential; it showed her delicateness and discretion, and was associated, therefore, with her femininity: "Mexican women are slaves to the rules of etiquette and they scrupulously observe the rules of propriety" (Kolonitz 1984, 114).

Various sources point to the importance of family ties for women, as well as the rituals that reinforced these ties: Kolonitz notes that "[i]n Mexico, family relationships are among the most intimate. Relations between parents and children, between sisters and brothers, are extremely affectionate. . . . Girls, when they marry, do not enter their husband's house, and most of the time it is the husband who comes to be part of his wife's family. In this manner numerous sons and daughters gather around their progenitors" (ibid., 108).

Women's emotional dependence was consistent with the education they received, by which they were conditioned to subordination and obedience. Marriage was the ideal space for them to carry out what they had learned in childhood as well as to practice a "respectable" form of sexuality, the objective of which was motherhood. The following is a well-known prayer that was said before having intercourse:

> It is not out of vice
> nor is it out of fornication
> but to make a child
> in your holy service

Being unmarried was associated with being a virgin; if a girl was a candidate for marriage at the age of fourteen, by the age of thirty she was considered a spinster. Called an "old maid," she was often stereotyped in the pejorative and mocking expression "quedarse a vestir santos" (literally, "to be left to dress statues of saints"—equivalent to the English expression "to be left on the shelf"). Nevertheless, the traditional value of chastity must have been important, at least among certain sectors. Research is needed to determine to what degree "spinsters'" solitude could bring greater independence and how they were able to adapt to changes in social processes. If the convent ceased to be an option, where and how could unaccompanied women live?

Courtship was valued, since it was a key stage in a woman's life: the rituals associated with it filled young people of both sexes with expectation. It combined games of intrigue, secret messages, naïve love letters, and furtive looks with fear for having sinned. Maintaining sexual propriety was essential, otherwise a young women could lose her reputation—indispensable for obtaining a good husband. It was important that girls obey the women's "commandments":

1. Do not deceive one's mother.
2. Do not trade the flower of innocence for the favor and scorn of any man.
3. Do not prefer silk and diamonds to the well-being of one's family.
4. Do not see flattery or flirtation as a path for acquiring popularity.
5. Do not gossip.
6. Do not speak in a loud voice or use bold mannerisms to call attention to oneself.
7. Do not study more with one's feet than with one's head.
8. Do not drink anything but water or go around with those who drink other than water.
9. Do not neglect the service to God, the creator of all things.
   (*El hogar* 1872, 123)

The recommendations taken by Sahagún from the remote pre-Columbian past appear not to have been very distant from these.

Courtship was governed by custom: "A young man who for some time has been courting a girl is taken to be her suitor, and even if they have not become engaged, he has the right to accompany her on her horseback rides during the promenade, to sit next to her in the carriage . . . or in the theater, to defend her and accompany her wherever necessary. It is not looked on with disapproval that the girl distribute her small favors or smiles to several suitors and that she cordially encourage them or coldly reject them. In this, as well, Mexican men give proof of unlimited patience because their assiduousness normally lasts for several years, until the [young women] makes up her mind" (Kolonitz 1984, 109). Young men played a role that was subordinate, submissive, and depen-

dent on the acceptance of their maiden, although, once the die was cast—
that is, after the marriage ceremony—the roles switched: the married
woman's greatest virtues were abnegation and obedience, and she had to
be submissive, even regarding her husband's infidelities.

Women and Liberalism: From the Convent to School

In the early years of Mexican independence, women's education did not
undergo noteworthy changes; the lack of cultural stimulus was evident.
An important purpose of education was to prevent young girls from
coming into contact with the opposite sex, even with boys their own age.
Calderón (1970, 28) explains: "I do not think there are three married
women, or as many girls above fourteen in all Mexico, who, with the
exception of the mass book on Sundays and fête days, ever open a book
in the whole course of a year." They learned to paint, embroider, do
delicate needlework, play the piano and, frequently, speak French.
Education, determined by one's sex, excluded any precise knowledge of
sexuality. With keen insight, the marquise blames this shortsightedness
for the frequent decision of young girls to enter the convent, with the
expectation that they would thus ensure their salvation. They would
confine themselves to the cloister when they were too young to even
know about relations with men or the possibilities afforded through
learning. Calderón also believes they took the veil because they anx-
iously looked forward to the celebration of their profession and to the
dress they would wear on the day of their farewell to the world.

We lack precise data on the number of Mexican women who participated in religious life and on the conditions in which they lived in the
different regions, although Arrom (1985b) suggests that the provinces
followed the pattern set by the capital. As mentioned, convents obtained
money and power by managing urban and rural property and functioning
as moneylenders. They also received charitable donations.

With the Reforma, the state attempted to promote capitalism by
transferring church property to private parties. Consequently, clerical
property was sold, convents were closed, the Civil Registry Law was
passed, civil marriage was instituted, cemeteries were secularized, and
many religious feasts were eliminated.

The 1859 *exclaustración* law (Decloistering Law, by which nuns were
forced to leave the convents) limited the clergy's power and hindered the
development of some institutions, such as the houses of seclusion,
which had been beneficial for women.[8] The Sisters of Charity were not
affected by this provision because they did not live in community and
their purpose was to provide charitable "services for humanity." In 1861
hospitals and benevolent establishments were secularized, and civil

authorities were empowered to administer nuns' dowries.[9] The *exclaustración* law was promulgated on February 26, 1863; nuns were given eight days to vacate their convents, which then became state property.[10] In March a series of measures was published to prevent nuns from regrouping and resuming religious practices, such as living in community. The decrees stated they "shall enjoy all the rights that the country's laws grant to women, and they shall thus have the same obligations that [the law] imposes on them. . . . These women, regardless of their age, will necessarily submit to their father, like all unmarried persons of their sex"; if they have no father and are legal adults, "they will be free to make use of their person and their interests and consequently they may choose their [place of] dwelling[;] . . . if they have a mother they shall live in the house of the latter."[11] We do not know what happened to these women in the years that followed.

The thinkers of the Reforma encouraged instruction for both sexes, since one of the tenets of liberalism was the creation of equal opportunities so that the most capable individuals would excel, and this, in turn, entailed giving everyone the freedom to learn. Around 1860, Ignacio Ramírez (1960, 2:189) defended the premise that women should have an education similar to that of men, so that they could become more efficient mothers: "Public, scientific, positive education will not be general and perfect until it begins in the family; nature did not intend for women to be mothers for [a purpose] other than that they be governesses." Hence they were assigned the role of endorsing the system from the home, by using their affection to influence their children in line with the country's needs, and by employing their sensitive, warm "nature" and their instinct to comfort the tired fighter from the public world.

Education, in addition, would integrate women into the nation, into the civilian and secular country the Reforma hoped to bring about, given the church's erstwhile strong influence. Benito Juárez established the obligation of the state to provide free, secular, and compulsory education. In 1861, the teaching of catechism was eliminated in schools, although in practice traditional customs prevailed (Bermúdez 1988, 127–152). Nor did Maximilian's 1865 reform remain in effect long enough to modify classroom practices and customs. Ignacio Ramírez's statement (1960, 187) was still a wish: "God does not distinguish between men and women." This pointed to the spirit that would govern *porfirismo*, the world of science in which it was possible to mock the idealism that denied women the possibility of becoming enlightened in the interest of safeguarding their delicate gender: "Romanticism is a luxury and it agrees poorly with poverty and ignorance; the romanticism of a foolish girl costs a couple of pesos in any suspicious establishment" (ibid., 189).

Women's education had not yet attempted to change the ideals surrounding women; rather, it sought only to better prepare them. This attitude would remain during the period of Porfirio Díaz. Ignacio Ramírez expresses this thinking as follows:

> We shall not deal with [the topic of] women as they have existed in centuries past, machines of pleasure in some nations[;] machines to make children and dresses and food in others; and in most, a positive piece of luxury furniture for the rich and a dependent, the first among domestic animals, for the poor.
> Nor shall we consider them in the future desired by the most audacious reformers: equal to men in teaching posts, in tribunals, at the rostrum and possibly even on the battlefields. We shall examine women just as today they illuminate our home, shine at banquets and at dances, descend from the altar to form a new family and are conclusively classified by divine and human laws. (Ibid., 186)

Two depictions of La Malinche and Córtez from the *Lienzo de Tlaxcala*.
Courtesy of the Benson Latin American Collection.

Virgin of Guadalupe. Courtesy of the Benson Latin American Collection.

Yucatán tortilla maker.
Courtesy of the Benson Latin
American Collection.

Zapotecan Indian. Courtesy
of the Benson Latin American Collection.

Casimiro Castro: Mexicanas' dress. Courtesy of UNAM.

Carlos Nebel: Villagers. Courtesy of UNAM.

Conceptionist nun, late 1700s. Photo by Palle Pallesen Christensen, courtesy of Colección Museo Nacional del Virreinato, INAH.

Nuns of New Spain in their habits. Courtesy of the Benson Latin American Collection.

Sor Juana Inés de la Cruz. Courtesy of the Benson
Latin American Collection.

María Guadalupe Ramírez, age 12 (1787).
Courtesy of the Benson Latin American
Collection.

Hesiquio Iriarte: The upstairs maid. Courtesy of UNAM.

José Guadalupe Posada: Collection of Love Letters. Courtesy of UNAM.

MAICERIA.

Los Lamentos de las Tortilleras.

Llanto y angustia ha causado
del maíz la gran carestía,
porque se ve de día á día
el pueblo más apurado.

Gran bulla y mucho alboroto
hay por la escasez del maíz,
y hacen las gentes un voto
para no comer á raíz.

Las humildes tortilleras
Hoy se dan codo con codo,
Dicen se ha perdido todo
Horita sí vá deveras.
Que haremos las molenderas,
De altiro la han amolado
Con lo que nos ha pasado,
Arruinadas de remate,
En descanso está el metate
Y mi viejo no ha almorzado.

No te atlijas mariguana,
Le dice su valedor,
La cosa no está tan pior
Por el barrio de Santana,
Y vete muy de mañana
A buscar la sucursal,
Por allí está tio Pascual
El te dará la linterna,
Donde lo venden sin merma,
Y con medida cabal.

Y la pobre de María
Se encamina muy al trote
Sin darle á los pies garrote
En su rápida tranvía.
Y llega a la maicería
Entrando en el pelotón,
Y recibe un estrajón
Al entrar en el mitote,
Y luego con el garrote
Dan ¡premio á su apuración.

Mas por fin, logra meterse
Atenida á sus codillos,
Y grita cuatro cuartillos
Que el nixtamal no se cuese.
Casi sin poder moverse
Va poniendo el chiquihuite
Y á cada instante repite,
Despácheme D. Pascual
Que se me quema el comal
Y tengo que hacer mi esquite.

José Guadalupe Posada: The complaints of the tortilla sellers. Courtesy of UNAM.

4

Peace in Porfirian Times
In the Maelstrom of "Progress"

⊁⊀

Between Two Centuries

In 1876, a Liberal, Porfirio Díaz, rose up against President Sebastián Lerdo de Tejada, who subsequently resigned, allowing Díaz to take office in 1877. Following the brief interregnum (1880–1884) of his *compadre* Manuel González, Díaz returned to the presidency and would have himself reelected for six more terms. The period of his rule (1877–1911) is known as *porfirismo* or the *porfiriato*, and it appeared to end the recurrent political upheaval and instability.

During the *porfiriato*, Mexico used its much-longed-for peace to grow. This growth was not a new national project, but the first potentiality of implementing Liberal ideas that had emerged since the late eighteenth century, something the Reforma finally made possible. The process was slow, materializing at the end of the nineteenth century and the beginning of the twentieth. Foreign capital entered the country, and France was considered the pinnacle of culture and the arts. Gradually, factories were built and commerce expanded; the network of railways increased from 285 miles in 1877 to 12,000 miles in 1919, and the financial system developed considerably.

This long, thirty-four-year period of *porfirismo* brought both change and continuity. Initially the government sought to consolidate political and military institutions, and, as the state became stronger, it emphasized efficacious administration and economic growth. The positivist ideology of Auguste Comte was adopted during this period. The regime's leaders were called *científicos* (scientists), to distinguish them from the churchmen who had dominated previous eras. Liberal ideas shaped economic policies, and the slogans "peace, order, and progress" and "little politics and much administration" served as guidelines for official policy. The ruling class hoped to build a modern country, despite the continued influence of tradition and the Catholic Church, especially regarding popular thinking. The idea of revolution as a way to achieve progress was abandoned in favor of the "evolution of social life." The Darwinist principle of the survival of the fittest was applied to social matters, and the different human groups were defined according to their purported "nature."

Discourse on women focused on two basic aspects of their supposed nature: their biology and their affective temperament. Both circumscribed women's destiny to motherhood and their occupation to that of being housewives. These tenets were now couched in "scientific" terms. In a variety of ways, and most notably in medical discourse, motherhood was exalted: women whose bodies did not fulfill that expectation were thought to have gone to waste, and chastity was scorned.

Women's traditional contradictions were heightened during this era. The following examples were particularly evident:

1. The discourse of the schools, the church, and the state defined women by their sex, their reproductive role; nevertheless, because modesty was expected to be their greatest adornment, the same institutions prevented them from learning about sex and reproduction.

2. Women were considered inferior because their reasoning was supposedly limited by biology, although their lack of ambition, their affective capacity, and their predilection for menial labor supposedly made them morally superior.

3. Housework was valued less and less because more products were sold for domestic use; nevertheless, it was felt that women could advance only within the home. Gooch (1887, 208) noted that "ladies have the advantage in the house; for even if the President were to call, the lady of the house is not expected to rise from her seat to receive him."

4. Although women were expected to make their home the center of their lives, the economic system forced many of them to leave their private domain in order to find work.

In sum, a contradiction unfolded: femininity was increasingly sublimated, while at the same time flesh-and-blood women were marginalized and kept in an inferior position. The marked social inequality of this period meant few could live the ideals presented to them. Most women experienced a glaring contradiction between their private lives and what was deemed ideal behavior. The latitude for choosing different life options was narrowed, and, consequently, women hoped for change and did their best to bring it about.

In the legal sphere, the 1870 Civil Code for the Federal District and Territories of Baja California, with strong Napoleonic influence, consolidated the Liberal model. Women were subordinated to their husbands, who administered their property and whose permission they needed in order to work. Male authority extended to children. Although the code permitted legal separation, divorce still did not dissolve marriage bonds. Many feared divorce would be detrimental to women, who supposedly found protection and sustenance in marriage. In 1884 the code was amended slightly (Arrom 1985a). Still, the underlying assumption of both versions of the code was that women were weak and needed men's support.

Women were expected to take care of themselves and their homes, yet they assumed a greater public role because this benefited the new system of "order and progress." Whereas women of the popular classes increasingly took jobs in factories (textile and tobacco, mainly), middle-class women showed more and more interest in education.

Whereas in the nineteenth century most working women were employed as maids or seamstresses, during the *porfiriato*, this began to change. Gradually they were hired as store clerks, secretaries, and stenographers. In 1885, 183,293 women, or 26.5 percent of the economically active population, worked. By 1890 this number had risen to 210,566, and the number of women wage earners surpassed that of domestic servants (Vallens 1986, 44). The 1900 census indicated that the population had increased to 13,607,259; 210,556 women worked in factories and 188,061 as domestic servants (Lau and Ramos 1993, 355).

Schools were opened where women could receive professional training. In 1890, the Escuela Normal para Señoritas (Women's Normal School) was founded. In 1892, the Escuela de Artes y Oficios (School for the Arts and Trades) was established, and by the end of the century it had more than one thousand students. In 1903, the Escuela Mercantil Miguel Lerdo de Tejada opened its doors. More women were becoming primary schoolteachers and more were studying. Between 1886 and 1889 the first woman dentist, surgeon, and lawyer graduated (Vidales 1980, 246). Gooch (1887, 236) relates, "During my sojourn at the capital, one young señorita graduated in dentistry. She began at once assisting her father, who was a dentist, in his office, the fact being announced in all the leading daily papers"—as if, she appears to say, this were an extraordinary event.

The percentage of women workers in the new factories increased, and women began to hold jobs in public offices and stores, where women clerks were seen more and more frequently. Nevertheless, women continued to be the heart and soul of the home, and the inspiration and subject of poets. Even the testimonies of workers conveyed the notion that the ideal woman was a domestic object, and they criticized the conditions that made it necessary for women to enter the factory and neglect their own domain. Hence, they recognized the incompatibility of their needs as a class and the ideological needs of traditional social morality. A woman who used the name "Eva" wrote "The Mission of Women" in the periodical *El hijo del trabajo* (The son of work), stating:

> In the nineteenth century[,] in which positivism is attempting
> to kill poetry . . . some women[—]few, fortunately![—] appear to
> be attacked by a sort of illness that could be called the dizziness
> of freedom. In them . . . [we see] open rebellion against all the
> laws of nature. Rather than limiting themselves to the rightful
> ambition of becoming men's equals through enlightenment and
> talent . . . they want to appropriate the right to give orders, a
> right that God has reserved to the strong sex. Oh! They ought to
> remember that there exists for women a more noble mission
> than that of striving to obtain the freedom to vote and to sit
> among legislators in order to govern a nation, when they have to
> govern their house. Rather than demanding some rights, the
> usage of which would be harmful for some, impossible for
> others, and ridiculous for most, they ought to remember
> woman's sweet mission: to love and console! When God created
> the first woman of humankind, he gave her to man not as a
> slave, not as a tyrant, but, instead, as a companion. (CEHSMO
> 1975, 11–12)

Even among workers, views on women were ambivalent because, just
as today, women's social role alluded to spheres that went beyond social
classes. Even women experienced this confusion and contradiction, as
"Eva's" writing shows:

> If we are inferior to man; if, like him, we cannot always use
> [our] free will; if we cannot, like him, wet our lips with that
> intoxicating liquor called freedom, we also possess some advan-
> tages that at times make us morally superior to men. . . . let us
> leave them the authority that all divine and human laws have
> conferred on them. . . . if men give glory, we give happiness.
> (Ibid.)

Industry owners paid this new worker between one-third and one-half
the wage received by men, although this varied from region to region and
factory to factory (Keremitsis 1973). In 1898, in Río Blanco—Mexico's
Manchester—children earned between 30 and 50 centavos per day,
women received between 60 and 80 centavos, and men, between 56
centavos and 2.50 pesos. In demanding greater social justice, Ricardo
Flores Magón asked for a minimum wage of 75 centavos per day for men,
40 centavos for women, and 30 centavos for children (ibid., 200).[1]
Workdays also varied among factories or regions, but a normal workday
lasted around twelve hours (ibid., 204).

Although the overall number of women who worked in the textile industry is difficult to ascertain, by 1880, of an estimated 1,073 employees in cotton factories, 384 were women and 227 were children (ibid., 209). Working conditions for women in these factories appear to be representative of the exploitation they suffered in other industries, such as the tobacco or the garment sectors.

Although many women worked before marrying, some married women also worked double workdays. In a situation defined by both their class and their gender, they worked as they always had, but more of them began to do so with a new, fundamental nuance: they entered the world of production, of wages. Hence, the difference between the public and private became more pronounced. Undoubtedly, working within the home, as women had always done—even when making products such as handcrafts or prepared food—was different from going outside the home, having to comply with a schedule and rules of conduct that frequently required leaving children alone or with elder relatives. Women helped create the conditions that allowed them to recognize they belonged to a given social class, minimizing the influence of institutions such as the church that downplayed class consciousness. Now their own work, not that of their father or husband, placed them within a specific group. Women who worked for wages could broaden their vision of the world and transcend the relatively narrow boundaries of their homes, as well as experiment with erstwhile unknown types of participation and power.

This change was significant, even though only a small number of women—but more than in previous times—were now working for wages. This process reflected the particular manner in which dependent countries became incorporated into world capitalism: rather than surpassing prior modes of production, dependent countries superimposed the new modes of production on an unequal system. Most women continued to work in the private sphere, inside the home, and in a position of inferiority, as their ancestors had, that is, in productive and reproductive labor, doing chores and making handcrafts, but immersed in the family unit, and, therefore, without a wage. Although the conditions of rural women varied from region to region, the lives of women of the popular classes were almost always arduous, both because of the lack of technology and because of a tradition in which violence against women appears to have been widespread.[2]

Moreover, prostitution was common. In 1905, out of Mexico City's population of 368,000, 11,554 prostitutes were registered with the Health Department, that is, 120 of every 1,000 women. In the same year, 4,371 prostitutes were detained for working without the permission of the health authorities. Prostitutes' ages ranged from fifteen to thirty; hence this problem affected a large number of young people (Turner

1967, 606), although it also demonstrated a long-standing double standard.

During the *porfiriato,* prostitution was strictly regulated. Prostitutes had to submit to a weekly checkup and carry a card, as well as pay a tax according to their category, which was determined by their place of work (they could either be "community" or independent workers) or by their personal traits (attractive, average figure, homely).[3]

Stephen Crane, an American traveler, journalist, and novelist, felt that

> The Mexican women are beautiful frequently but there seems to
> be that quality lacking which makes the bright quick eyes of
> some girls so adorable to the contemplative sex. It has some-
> thing to do with the mind, no doubt. Their black eyes are as
> beautiful as gems. The trouble with the gem however is that it
> cannot regard you with sudden intelligence, comprehension,
> sympathy. They have soft rounded cheeks which they powder
> without much skill, leaving it often in streaks. They take life
> easily, dreamily. They remind one of kittens asleep in the
> sunshine. (Katz 1970, 67)

Another characteristic of *porfirismo* was entertainment, frivolousness—the flip side of "order and progress." If French influence was evident in fashion, in ideas, and in the affected use of Molière's language among the middle and upper classes, it was not universal: "[I]n these places of popular theater and shows, in this ambiance of music and stages, it is possible to accuse the *porfiriato* of excessive Frenchification. [However,] the refined Gallic influences did not permeate the scandalous peripheries of popular music and dances" (Dallal 1987, 74). A carefree, lighthearted atmosphere existed alongside the elites' ballroom dances, opera, and high culture.

Frivolous customs proliferated in these popular milieus, and the authorities attempted to control them; dragnets against homosexuals (like one in which forty-one homosexuals were banished to Yucatán) were famous, as was police intervention in brawls that often followed unrestrained revelries, more common in the early years of this century (ibid., 76). Motion pictures also found a public, as did entertainment that targeted single men (Reyes 1973, 94 ff). Performances at the Principal and Guerrero theaters featured merry, provocative, suggestively attired women singing risqué lyrics and even dancing the cancan! Buxom performers such as María Conesa, the "white kitten," who came to Mexico in 1908, intrigued the public, and purportedly scandalized high society. These performances continued during the Revolution and the "maximato,"[4] although in the latter period they, peculiarly, began to touch on political topics.

Several innovations changed the tone of life: the railroad had helped shape a new country; cities were more comfortable; electricity, the phonograph, telephone, motion pictures, and typewriters became accessible. One sector of urban society found the world more amenable. Modes of transportation included the bicycle, the streetcar, and, gradually, the automobile. Perhaps the reduction in animal-drawn vehicles even modified the smell of the cities.

Once again ideologues emphasized the need to educate women to be better wives and mothers, and for defenseless women to avoid prostitution. In the classroom, middle-class women found a new possibility for survival and for what was considered dignified work, and women teachers raised a series of fundamental questions regarding women's condition.

Although primary education was compulsory, in practice the law could not be enforced. In 1878 the Regulation for Girls' Primary and Secondary Schools was unveiled, as was that for boys' schools in 1879. Girls were not taught history or civics, but they were instructed in "obligations of the woman in society and of the mother in her relations with the family and state," as well as in hygiene and home medicine. Civics was taught only to girls studying to be teachers, so they could teach this subject to their future male pupils. In coming years, women teachers would display their patriotic spirit and propose important social and legal changes for women.

The Emergence of Feminism

Middle-class and working-class women had more public presence and therefore more opportunity to become aware of gender and class issues. By producing wealth rather than merely having children or cleaning houses, they also became more familiar with their country and, therefore, learned about and participated in social organizations and movements. *Porfirismo* ushered in a period of great activity among women—including feminist activities. Women participated both in broad-based social movements as well as in movements that specifically addressed gender demands. The feminism of this period stressed the respect that women deserved and the characteristics considered intrinsic to them, such as sweetness and emotivity. Women were considered superior to men, and it was felt that education would allow women to become fully cognizant of their reality. The feminist movement made society aware of women's issues, although at an extremely slow pace. Women teachers were the main protagonists in this struggle, since their role in the work force made them aware of the indisputable inequality between men and women and caused them to become precursors of change as pioneers of the feminist cause.

Women workers also had a significant role. The First Workers Congress (1876) focused on the need to improve conditions for working women, to a large degree because of concern about the double workday and the consequent neglect of children. Nevertheless, the Congress refused to receive a delegation of women, arguing that women lacked legal status. The record of the proceeding notes the presence of "two likable young ladies, worthy of the highest honor because of their talent, because of their love for the working classes" (CEHSMO 1975, 199). Still, these virtues were deemed insufficient, since "propriety prohibits letting women participate in public tasks. . . . A woman's stage is her home; her mission as mother and educator not only of the family but of humankind is already [too] high for us to distract her from it, for us to, in disturbing the order of nature, replace her mission of calming storms, of putting the sweet note in life with that of hardening [life], [causing] her to take on struggles which frequently erupt in impulsive passions, and in which even the most serene and least distraught and the least agitated spirits normally harbor their contingent of bitterness" (ibid.). A gender-specific oppression became evident, regardless of a woman's social class: the proper place for all women was the home, where they were supposedly protected from passions.

The Second Workers Congress (1880) was presided over by Carmen Huerta, a (male) leader of textile workers who some historians believed to be a woman (Rascón 1979, 152). Women had already played a clear role in the struggles and strikes carried out by textile workers in Mexico City. Despite the short-term failure, this feminine sector began to prepare itself within social praxis. Historical accounts tell us that Margarita Martínez and Lucrecia Toriz (an illiterate mother of twenty-two children) sparked the movement that led to the 1906 Río Blanco strike, considered a necessary antecedent of the 1910 Revolution.

Very much in line with the Liberal premise that the press is a catalyst of social change, some women's magazines traced their roots to Rita Cetina Gutiérrez, who in 1870 had published La siempreviva (The everlasting [flower]), and to the authors of Hijas del Anáhuac (Daughters of Anáhuac), published in Mexico City in 1873. The paper and ink of these publications were used for the feminist cause. The most noteworthy examples are Albúm de la mujer: Periódico redactado por señoras (The woman's album: Newspaper written by married women), headed by the Spaniard Concepción Gimeno de Flaquer, from 1883 to 1889, and Violetas del Anáhuac, edited by Laureana Wright de Kleinhans and later by Mateana Murguía, from 1887 to 1888. These texts accurately expressed a feminism that strove for social recognition for women and that insisted on their need for secular education so they could carry out their socially assigned roles more effectively and with greater self-esteem, but without altering those roles. Accordingly, Laureana Wright wrote "La emancipación de la mujer por medio del estudio" (Woman's emancipation through study; 1905) and *Mujeres notables mexicanas* (1910), published after her death, which accurately described the origins of this branch of feminism.

At the dawn of the century, Dolores Correa Zapata, Laura Méndez de Cuenca, and Mateana Murguía published the magazine *La Mujer Mexicana*.[5] In the February 14, 1904, issue, Mexico's first woman lawyer, María Sandoval de Zarco, wrote that the editors' goal was to bring about "the physical, intellectual and moral improvement of women, the cultivation of sciences, fine arts and industry, the mutual assistance of the members of said society." In 1905, this same group of women formed the Society for the Protection of Women.

Feminist ideas were shared by Genaro García, an important thinker and historian of this period. In 1891, he wrote *Apuntes sobre la condición de la mujer* (Notes on women's condition) and *La desigualdad de la mujer* (The inequality of women), in which he called for legal equality of the sexes.

Other advocates of legal equality in the early years of the century included the aforementioned Society for the Protection of Women and the Cosmos Women's International Society. A more politically oriented group, the Admirers of Juárez (founded in 1904) advocated women's right to vote in 1906. Throughout the country, groups and clubs were formed that would eventually work with the opponents of Porfirio Díaz to prevent his reelection. Women in this movement—about whose lives we are beginning to learn more—include: Inés Malváez, Luz Vera, Hermila Galindo, Eulalia Guzmán, Dolores Jiménez y Muro, Juana Belén Gutiérrez de Mendoza, and Elisa Acuña y Rosetti.

During the more than fifteen years in which Juana Belén Gutiérrez published the weekly magazine *Vésper*, she suffered multiple vicissitudes and persecutions, which at times forced her to change the name of her publication and even to serve time in jail. Her perseverance never wavered, however, and she was an indefatigable organizer of women's groups. *Vésper* was essential to the development of feminist thought in Mexico. Gutiérrez founded *Vésper* in Guanajuato in 1901, with the motto "Justice and Liberty," to defend miners and oppose the clergy. In 1902, in Mexico City, she came into contact with groups opposed to the government and subscribed to libertarian ideas. In 1903, Gutiérrez and Elisa Acuña were listed as directors of the Club Liberal Ponciano Arriaga.

Around 1910, the thinkers of the Partido Liberal Mexicano (PLM;

Mexican Liberal Party) became radicalized and espoused anarchism. The party's leaders, the brothers Ricardo and Enrique Flores Magón, edited the newspaper *Regeneración. Magonismo* aimed chiefly at improving labor conditions; it was very strong in northern Mexico and closely tied to Mexican and U.S. groups in the southwestern United States (California, Arizona, Texas). Although their concerns clearly related more to labor issues than to feminist ones, women were included in their demands and in their leadership. Among these leaders were Sara Estela Ramírez, nicknamed the "Red Rose," Andrea Villarreal, and María Talavera, as well as some American women, such as Mary Harris Jones, Elizabeth Darling Trowbridge, and Luella Twinning (Rocha 1991, 214–221).[6] The PLM's 1906 platform called for equality between men and women and for the regulation of domestic work.

In 1910, in *Regeneración*, Ricardo Flores Magón wrote "A la mujer," inviting women to join the revolutionary struggle (ibid., 224–228). This call was heard by some women textile workers in Tizapán, including the sisters María del Carmen and Catalina Frías, who along with Juana Belén Gutiérrez de Mendoza organized the Hijas de Anáhuac (Daughters of Anáhuac), a group of some three hundred women workers (CEHSMO 1975, 20) who sympathized with the Mexican Liberal Party.[7] For its part, the PLM drew its membership from the working class and the petty bourgeoisie, and some of its demands would become the foundation for the social doctrines of the 1917 Constitution. These women called for a maximum eight-hour workday, a minimum wage, safety norms, and the regulation of domestic work (ibid.).

Feminism's concerns grew and were expressed through organizations, magazines, and, especially, the work of a group of women whom we must acknowledge as the pioneers of the struggle for the emancipation of Mexican women.

The End of an Era

Poverty and inequality were obvious by the end of the *porfiriato*. As is often the case, descriptions by foreigners highlighted conditions that Mexicans had become so accustomed to that they no longer noticed. Some German journalists pointed out the social contrast in the very commercial center of Mexico City between "women with simple dark shawls and a thick layer of dust on their yellow faces[, and] ladies in elegant dresses, which they coquettishly lift above their small white feet in white shoes, and who leave behind a layer of strong perfume. Women in impeccable dark frock coats [with] a flower in the buttonhole[, alongside,] once again, indigenous women, who, in ragged skirts . . . [are seen] walking, or, rather, silently dragging their feet on the marble tile, [while] through the holes of their shirts their brown breasts show" (Monjarás-Ruiz 1975, 38).

These Germans were surprised that among the popular classes extreme poverty coexisted with vanities in adornment and devotion; this social morality clashed with the pragmatism of their own country. Hence, in the *cantinas* and on the dirty streets, in the poor, dusty houses, they were astonished to see paintings of saints framed in gold, or "dark old hags who make tortillas and scold the children, wearing only what is essential, although often with earrings hanging from their ears" (ibid., 39). The customs of the times were clearly ambiguous; in the same urban center, postcards were sold that showed "sinful variety show stars with very low-necked [blouses], and other [cards] with pious women communicants who carry rosaries, cheap toys and costume jewelry" (ibid., 39). On this topic, Stephen Crane noted, interestingly: "I refuse to commit judgment upon these lower classes of Mexico. I even refuse to pity them. It is true that at night many of them sleep in heaps in doorways, and spend their days squatting upon the pavements. It is true that their clothing is scant and thin . . . but yet their faces have almost a certain smoothness, a certain lack of pain, a serene faith. I can feel the superiority of their contentment" (Bergon 1979, 220–221).

An awareness of social contradictions obliged some Mexican intellectuals to seek solutions. In 1908, Andrés Molina Enríquez wrote *Los grandes problemas nacionales* and raised the need to redistribute large agricultural landholdings. His positivist tenets led him to seek organic, scientific explanations for the issues he researched; hence, he offered a biologically skewed interpretation of the makeup of the family. His position, which harks back to the views of Auguste Comte, is important, since positivism was the ruling-class ideology at the end of the *porfiriato*, and we can assume that it strongly influenced all of society.

Molina Enríquez, drawing on Ernst Haeckel (*Natural History of Creation*, 1868), thought men have an overriding physical need to eliminate what he called "cellular aggregates" (accumulated sperm); otherwise serious organic disorders will result, including stunted growth. Given his belief in this biological, sexual need, Molina drew up a gender-based social hierarchy: men are incomplete because they cannot reproduce; women are also incomplete because they "lack the aptitude to support themselves in an unequal work struggle with men" (1972, 177). Hence, because of their greater ability and strength, men's basic social role is to provide food. Women are weaker, for which reason, "their [bodies,] devoted to inactive functions, offer the laziness and roundness that for us constitute beauty" (ibid., 178). Consequently, they "cannot obtain their food except by the hand of man, and men cannot expel their cellular aggregates other than through women" (ibid.). When women join the work force, this balance is upset and society as a whole is affected by the modification of reproductive patterns—as is, therefore, the construction of the family as a system, which has "the father as head, the mother as the person subordinated to the father, and the children dependent on the mother and submitted like her to the head of the family" (ibid., 184).

Molina Enríquez attempted, then, to give a biological foundation to women's lower social position. He was surprised by theories that maintained that the family institution was based on social needs (ibid.), and he vigorously defended his model. Molina Enríquez, considered ahead of his time in social theory, was nevertheless behind the times regarding women's issues, and he put a scientific veneer on old premises. Last, we must acknowledge the importance of religion, which allowed this prestigious positivist thinker to state: "Woman . . . [was] formed from the very body of man, as biblical tradition states in all precision" (ibid., 180).

5

From Revolution to Stability

꒰꒱

Adelitas and *Marietas*

In 1910, Porfirio Díaz was reelected president for his sixth consecutive term. This time, however, was different. A change in leadership was demanded by the diminutive Francisco I. Madero—and Madero prevailed.

Discontent had been expressed since the beginning of the century with the PLM's petitions and demand that the election results be respected. Hence, women's insistence on being allowed to vote is not surprising. The Mexican Revolution was a complex, bloody movement in which various groups took part, each making its own claims. Among the different demands, those by and for women followed a distinctive path. The struggle that engulfed the country from 1910 to 1920 had repercussions not only in politics but also in the daily habits of men and women alike.

The anti-reelection movement begun by Madero culminated in 1911 with Porfirio Díaz's resignation and exile. The following year, Madero was ousted in a coup d'état led by General Victoriano Huerta. Emiliano Zapata in the south and Francisco Villa and Venustiano Carranza in the north, in turn, overthrew Huerta, before fighting among themselves to defend their own positions. Victory, at this stage, belonged to Carranza, who considered himself the legitimate successor to the presidency. His claim was buttressed by the promulgation of the 1917 Constitution, which is still in effect today.

Danger and ruthlessness marked the entire decade: all the leaders of the Revolution met violent deaths. Nor were the 1920s—the roaring and conflictive twenties—much more peaceful, although those at the helm of the state clearly tried to resolve the conflicts. First Álvaro Obregón and later Plutarco Elías Calles attempted to direct political activity toward institutions and political, legal, and economic arrangements.

The 1910 Revolution burst on Mexican history, clamoring for new options. It allowed participation by the popular classes, and it was precisely this participation that determined its basic course. The Revolution was a peasant movement led by a middle class that was suspicious and unhappy with the few possibilities for improvement afforded it during the *porfiriato*. The triumph of those who mainly desired to find a place in the power structure meant that the proposals of the popular classes were distorted and their demands manipulated. The same occurred regarding women's issues.

The Revolution ushered in the twentieth century, and the events that occurred during it have continued to leave an imprint on the nation's reality, since all successive governments have considered themselves its heirs. Women supported all factions in the war, and their participation has determined many of the paths that they, as social subjects, have followed since. Daily life was precarious for women, and abduction and rape were commonplace. Consequently, many women, especially the well-off, fled the country. Given the need to find safety, migration from the countryside to the city or vice versa—depending on the region—was also common.

Women's presence in the Revolution was so pervasive that their image has become part of the mythology surrounding the events of 1910. *Soldaderas* (a term that includes both women soldiers and camp followers) are key figures in the collective memory and they, like other subjects, have been stereotyped. The image of the *soldadera* has been consistent with the traditional archetypes of abnegation and sweetness, although a sexual overlay has been added. This stereotyping, like a stiff handmade doll, threatens to rob us of the warmth and complexity inherent to all social actors. We must remember that women's participation took many forms, and avoid the fixed idea of submissiveness and docility applied to the woman who followed her "Juan." Moreover, there has been a temptation to see the women of the Revolution, perhaps more than those of other historical moments, through a heroic lens that delights in photographs in which they appear with rifles and bandoliers. Some women dressed as men so they could take part in the struggle; some were troop commanders; but most had a less prominent, although not necessarily less important, role.

Women took part in many and in varied manners: the *New York Times* pointed out as early as the first year of the conflict (May 10, 1911) that "women have assumed a fundamental role in the Revolution."[1] They did so in multiple ways, and though they have generically been called *soldaderas* or *galletas* (literally, "cookies"), they went beyond the traditional portrayal of "a girl who courageously followed [the troops]/ wildly in love with the sergeant," immortalized in the popular song "La Adelita." *Soldaderas* earned respect because of their own contributions, and thus the song continues:

> popular among the troops was Adelita
> the woman whom the sergeant idolized
> since, in addition to being courageous, she was pretty
> and even the colonel respected her.

The admiration these women received is clear. In another ballad, one soldier confesses to Valentina, "I have thrown myself at your feet," since,

> if they are to kill me tomorrow
> [then] let them go ahead and kill me.

An American document, *Reel Life,* quoted in *Con Villa en México* by Aurelio de los Reyes, describes women's participation as follows:

> There is a class of Mexican women—by far the largest class—who do not stay at home. They experience not only war's ever-prolonged fear but for the safety of their loved ones, follow on the very heels of the troopers, live the hard lives of the men in camp and on the move, and in final sacrifices, even pour out their blood on the firing line. (*Reel Life* 1914, 10)

The text adds that women had to prepare the meals because there was no canned food: "A *soldadara* [sic] is given only the raw materials and she must put these together on quick notice when occasion demands" (ibid.). Still, these women often were not even given food to prepare the meals; they had to buy it, ask for it, or steal it. The *soldaderas'* presence can be explained, to a large degree, by the makeshift armies' inability to meet their daily needs. The text explains that a *soldadera* belonged to the army quartermaster corps and she moved close to the front line, although, at the same time, "she carries out the Red Cross spirit, for she will feed a hungry man of the enemy's ranks if she is sure he is a soldier" (ibid., 11). The document concludes with a foreboding paragraph:

> What is to happen next in Mexico is uncertain. What is sure is that Mexican women, from the lowest type of servile Indian to the lady of the best Castilian blood, are spirited and fearless and they may play a great part in the next years. (Ibid.)

Women clearly assumed the dangers and sorrows inherent to any war and took part on an equal footing and in accordance with their specificity. Women could carry and use the weapons made lighter by new technology, but they still carried out their traditional roles within the service sector of a precarious army that was unable to meet its needs effectively. Women tended the ill, cared for the children, and continued to give birth. They were present at the end of the day, when rest was in order after many hours of fighting or marching. For the most part, women maintained their traditional roles, although outside the individual or private domain, giving another dimension to women's tasks: the war forced women to work together with others, which, among some sectors, was quite usual. Hence, in makeshift kitchens, the ideal model of family privacy was broken, however much each woman was responsible for her own man and family. John Reed, the American journalist who witnessed the Revolution firsthand, recorded a conversation with two women who explained why they had joined the struggle. They complained: "Ah! it is a life for us *viejas* [a pejorative term, literally "old women," but not specific to any age group] . . . we follow our men out in the campaign, and then do not know from hour to hour whether they live or die" (1969, 169). One of the women notes that when she asked her companion if she should follow him in the *bola* (group of insurgents), he answered, "Shall I starve, then? Who shall make my *tortillas* for me but my woman?" (ibid.). Clearly, disarray in the revolutionary armies forced women to play their age-old role as service providers: cooks, launderers, and concubines, even though they also experimented with some new roles.

Writer Elena Poniatowska records the descriptions given by Jesusa Palancares of many experiences of women during the Revolution. Jesusa tells of joining the troops of Genovevo Blanco, who was accompanied by his daughter. "She was the general's daughter. I didn't talk with her. Only when we would arrive somewhere, there where she stayed, I would come close [to her]" (1984, 80). The general's status placed his daughter in a higher social class than Jesusa and set her apart from the rest of the men as well as from the women:

> At night she would walk around the camp and the men knew the sound of her boots:
> "Here she comes!"
> And they would quickly put the bottle away. But she could sense [that they were drinking] from miles away: "Someone give him a lashing." (ibid.)

As the daughter of an officer, she issued orders and had a prominent role:

> Everyone obeyed her. She would check all the men's aim. She would train the horses. She knew the caliber of the bullets and, with her father, she would plan attacks and defenses. "Clean the horses! Check the provisions! Put more straw on the cart! Get

all these scattered plebes together! Don't wander off!"

She was, however, very devout. At night she would kneel down and say the rosary, and under her shirt she wore not one, but three, scapulars. (Ibid., 80–81)

To lead in battle entailed a series of risks:

The general's daughter, Miss Lucía, pulled her own weight. When they would order: "Chests to the ground," she would throw herself to the ground like everyone else, and in this way she would advance and shoot her rifle. She never stayed back with the impedimenta. Neverly [sic]. I reckon she was an amazon. (Ibid., 80)

Jesusa does her best to explain life on the move, the organization of tents in which slept three or four single men or a family with children. During battle, children, along with their mothers, had to stay with the impedimenta:

There were almost no women in the campaigns, [my husband] Pedro brought me without the general's order . . . that's why I dressed up as a man[,] so they would overlook this. I covered my face with the bandana and [wore a] hat. Usually there were some [women] traveling like me[,] because their husbands forced them to, others, because they were pretending to be men, but most of the women would stay behind with the impedimenta. (Ibid., 109–110)

Jesusa would go into battle with her husband, and while he shot one Mauser, she would load the empty one for him (ibid., 110).

There were other women like her. Tomasa García, perhaps the most influenced by stereotypes of women, remembers:

They called us all "Adelitas" because we were revolutionaries, we were with the troops. But the real Adelita was from Ciudad Juárez.

That real Adelita would say, "C'mon, everyone get into this, and anyone who is afraid can stay and cook beans."

And bullets and more bullets [flew] and whoever didn't obey, she killed him herself! She was very courageous.

Juana Gallo . . . sold tacos, *garnachas* [meat pies] and everything among the troops; but she had a confrontation [and] that was where she joined. She did well. She was a natural at combating [*sic*] in combat and against bands of five or six.

Then there was Marieta. It's like [with] everything, if you're crazy, you give men their way. This Marieta was not up to fighting or taking a plaza. You come in [this] for combat, to fight mercilessly. To kill and to be killed! Marieta, she was good for driving all the troops crazy, very amorous!

There was also Petra, Soledá, many, most of us, all together, we were good at fighting! (Romo 1979, 13)

And their role was acknowledged. Women's participation in the army went against the ideal of the family model and even of fidelity, since, although a woman was generally the companion of one man, if he died, she looked for, and found, another. Nevertheless, this change could not take place automatically, and many rituals of conduct and courtship persisted. A popular song to Marieta advises her:

don't be flirtatious
because men are very evil
they promise many gifts
and what they give are nothing but beatings

Despite their customary violence, the men seem to have been able to show their affective dependence—perhaps because the immediate possibility of dying made it less necessary to fulfill the macho stereotype. They could sing at the top of their lungs that:

if Adelita left with another
I would follow her by land and by sea
if by sea[,] in a warship
if by land[,] in a military train

Men could not offer security or privacy, but only the doubt that if

I should die in a campaign
and they go to bury my body
Adelita[,] for God's sake[,] I beg
you to go shed your tears for me

Women had the option of being more than the pure and saintly sweethearts, traditional mothers, or wives. Turner writes that they "gained recognition as comrades, consorts and companions" (1967, 608).

The Revolution brutally incorporated women into public life, in the extreme harshness of a civil war. Women took part as couriers, spies, employees, arms and munitions runners, uniform and flag seamstresses, secretaries, journalists, nurses—all decision-making roles. Many women teachers strove to educate the troops, while others learned to use the telegraph. Women helped draft plans and manifestoes. Some observers have claimed that Dolores Jiménez y Muro wrote Porfirio Díaz's "Social Political Plan" in 1911. On some occasions, women—even prostitutes— also led heroic deeds. For example, a group in Veracruz, led by "América," shot at some American marines who had invaded the port's red-light district.[2] Women's presence transcended political divisions; women were included among the troops of Francisco Villa, Venustiano Carranza, Álvaro Obregón, and Emiliano Zapata.

These social actors participated in the struggle in two basic manners: as women, carrying out the task of obtaining provisions that had been traditional in Mexican armies or, as Ana Lau and Carmen Ramos (1993, 38) note, disguised as men: "In donning men's clothes, *soldaderas* leapt over the barriers, the limits that the gender arrangement imposed on them. They became men, if only momentarily. As combatants they had the same responsibilities as their male counterparts.... *Soldaderas* were rebels on two accounts: rebels against the regime's policies and rebels against their gender assignment."

Women on Different Sides . . . and in Different Places

Women's participation varied over time and according to the group to which they belonged. Although women generally joined the struggle freely, Huerta's army recruited both men and women through the levy (Turner 1967, 607–608).

Madero's movement inherited the anti-reelection struggle that had begun in the last years of the *porfiriato*. Both Madero and his wife, Sara P. de Madero, were active in this struggle and became models for political action. During this period, women's clubs proliferated. In 1909, Juana Belén Gutiérrez de Mendoza and Dolores Jiménez y Muro founded the Club Femenil Amigas del Pueblo (Friends of the People Women's Club), and joined Madero's cause. When the differences between Madero and Zapata became clear, both women sided with Zapata.

Another women's club, the Hijas de Cuauhtémoc, an offshoot of the Hijas de Anáhuac, predated Porfirio Díaz's departure. It organized a protest against the dictator and collected more than one thousand signatures (ibid.). The Hijas de Cuauhtémoc advocated women's moral, intellectual, physical, economic, and political equality. These demands were clearly based on the belief that equal options among social subjects would lead to real equality.

In these eventful years, various groups continued to affect the course of the struggle. The Club Lealtad (Loyalty Club), headed by María Arias Bernal, supported Madero's successful effort to oust Porfirio Díaz, and, true to their slogan ("Always faithful"), continued to back the Revolution's principles after Huerta executed Madero. Every Sunday they took flowers to Madero's grave, and they published an underground news bulletin on a portable printing press. In recognition of her courage, in 1914 Álvaro Obregón gave Arias Bernal his pistol. From then on, she was called Maríapistolas (María with pistols) (Soto 1990, 41).

Aurelio de los Reyes (1992, 110–111) points out that documentaries of those years portray women's organizations supporting Madero, waiting for him in train stations, giving speeches. Guilds also feted Madero: the tortilla makers of Puebla accompanied *"el chaparrito"* ("shorty") and his *sarape* (a play on words: his wife's name and middle initial, Sara P., pronounced quickly, sounds like *sarape*, Spanish for "blanket"). As the leader's wife, Sara de Madero readily supported the Revolution and her husband, and she is shown in movies encouraging the troops during battle and organizing rallies in support of the Revolution. The wives of Madero's successors were less involved in, if not completely detached from, the struggle, leaving politics to their husbands and seeking refuge in the quiet of their homes.

The fundamental demands of Emiliano Zapata and his followers were for land and respect for the autonomy of the *pueblos*. *Zapatismo* was influential in the states of Morelos, Guerrero, and Mexico, and it tended to remain within those boundaries, within which Zapata and his troops carried out guerrilla warfare. Because of the circumstances, women took part naturally, almost as if it were an extension of their daily work in their communities. Some held military rank; for example, Amelia Robles had herself called Colonel Amelio Robles and wore men's clothing, and Rosa Bobadilla was promoted to the rank of *coronela* upon her husband's death.

Since *zapatistas* were concerned with legality and social order, they proclaimed several laws: in 1915, they eliminated the distinction between legitimate and illegitimate children and they proposed a law to allow divorce. However, because the *zapatistas* were defeated, these laws were never put into practice; still, they are noteworthy, since they called attention to several social issues affecting men and women.

In the north, Francisco Villa's movement also incorporated women, but not in the same way as did the caudillo of the south, Zapata. In Villa's army, women seldom rose to positions of authority, and they were not allowed to express opinions on gender issues. Villa's movement was characterized by its mobility: his troops advanced from the northern border state of Chihuahua all the way to Mexico City. Many pictures of his troops in trains, which today we intrinsically associate with the

Revolution, and many songs considered part of Mexican folklore are from this period.

In Carranza's army, the Grupo Sanitario Acrata (Anarchist Health Group)—the women's branch of the Casa del Obrero Mundial (World Workers' House)—took up the standard of constitutional rule in 1915.[3] The distinction of *carrancismo*, among members of both sexes, was its concern with legal questions; its most belligerent and aggressive woman member was Hermila Galindo—Venustiano Carranza's secretary—who exerted a conscientious and decidedly feminist influence on the leader.

Importantly, hunger and economic crises often beset women who remained in the cities during the revolutionary years. Prostitution increased, poor sanitation bred epidemics, and instability became widespread. Moderately well-off families frequently suffered from sharply declining living standards that forced their daughters to accept powerful men as lovers for the protection they offered. In the deserted cities, variety shows and cinemas remained open, and since fashion magazines were no longer sold and women could no longer imitate Porifirio Díaz's wife, Doña Carmelita Romero Rubio de Díaz, they modeled their behavior on Italian divas: "there emerged the Menichellis, the Borellis, the Pina de Guadalupes and the Lidia Borreguis."[4] Aurelio de los Reyes (1981, 199) says that the divas were imitated down to their facial expressions: "[In Huerta's army,] 'society women' began to copy Borelli, and by 1916, this imitation had spread to broader social sectors, so that attire 'a la italiana' was commonplace among city women. Italian movies influenced a hungry and dreamy society." This imitation of fashion went beyond dresses and facial expressions: women dreamt of passion, of the amorous ardor that, according to rumor, was the daily fare for Pina Menichelli, Francesca Bertini, Lyda Borelli, and others. Photographs from that period show glamorous attire and poses, both in Mexico's society women and in its actresses, like Mimí Derba.

We might say the Revolution gave women as a group the opportunity to substantially change their social status. "In providing Mexican women with a new role in society and a new sense of national participation, the 1910 Revolution significantly altered the nature of nationalism and of society" (Turner 1967, 603). Naturally, some women used the opportunity to demand the necessary legal changes to improve their status.

Organizations, Congresses, and Laws

Feminist activity remained strong: women demanded the right to vote as early May 1911, and demanded that provisional President León de la Barra authorize it, arguing that the 1857 Constitution did not explicitly exclude women's suffrage. Organized protests often ended in violence. The press reported on similar struggles being waged by women in Europe and the United States, and some women even tried to imitate them in Mexican publications: From 1915 to 1919, Artemisa Sáenz Royo and Hermila Galindo, who was closely linked to Venustiano Carranza, edited *La Mujer Moderna: Semanario Ilustrado* (The modern woman: Illustrated weekly), which called for the enactment of women's suffrage. This issue advanced feminism beyond the nineteenth-century proposals, since feminists no longer considered themselves confined to the home and began to delve into politics, where they also hoped to use their clout through the ballot box.

Some revolutionary leaders had become aware of women's strength and potential: In addition to being in demand by factories and offices, women themselves had perceived the possibility of a different quality of life. A few women would continue the struggle to its logical conclusion. Others, admittedly, preferred familiar comfort; after all, feminism had emerged only recently, whereas ideological conditioning was ancestral.

The First Feminist Congress was called in 1915 in Tabasco by governor Francisco Múgica, a revolutionary general who espoused ideas of social improvement far ahead of his time. Despite scant information, we can consider the 1915 congress a precursor to those called by General Salvador Alvarado, a *constitucionalista* (that is, an ally of Venustiano Carranza). Alvarado was exceptional because of his advanced ideas and anti-clericalism. As governor of Yucatán (1915–1919), he said, "[U]ntil we raise women up it will be impossible for us to serve [our] country" (Turner 1967, 609). He felt that the church's influence on women would hinder the evolution of their thinking. To counter this, Alvarado called two feminist congresses in 1916, and the resulting resolutions influenced the Family Relations Law, which was included in the 1917 Constitution and supplanted the 1884 Civil Code. In the state of Yucatán, with a predominantly Indian population, progressive ideas circulated widely.

The first congress (in January) was attended by 617 delegates, mostly teachers, who stressed the need to raise educational standards for young women and to base schooling on secular principles, in order to help women overcome superstition and "religious fanaticism." In the second congress, in December, Hermila Galindo called for encouraging women to better understand their own bodies, since—she said—sexual desire is as strong in women as in men. The topic was given short shrift because it was considered offensive to the women present. A clear division emerged between those who held that social determination was sexually based and those concerned about the lack of knowledge regarding sex itself. The fear of change prevented progress. The same occurred with a petition to allow women to vote: although the issue was mentioned in the debates, it was not voted on and was filed away. Nevertheless, many statements regarding women were later incorporated in the 1917 Constitution.

The delegates were clearly naïve regarding the tactics and strategies needed by the women's struggle. Despite the governor's progressive credentials, his convocation of the congress was top-down, and grassroots consciousness was insufficient. Alaíde Foppa (1979, 56) writes, "The Congress in Yucatán, more than contributing ideas to the women's cause, reflected situations that, precisely, are a long way from breaking the *yoke of tradition*, but it also demonstrated that, in any situation, there are women willing to do something for their own cause" (Foppa's emphasis). We should add that some men are also more enlightened than others on these issues.

Governor Alvarado also issued several decrees to promote hiring women in the state administration; to implement the regulation of domestic work, requiring that servants be paid; to ban houses of prostitution; and to give women the legal right to leave their father's home at twenty-one years of age, a right their brothers already had. Naturally, these changes applied only to Yucatán.

Alvarado (1976, 143) wrote, "We now live, fortunately, in an era of women's emancipation. The absolute subservience of women to the predominance of men has passed into [history]. . . . Within the present-day sphere of real life, women are a social element with high responsibilities and inalienable rights." He believed that women could develop in both the family and the workplace "[a]s long as they have not associated with [a] man to form a family" (144). Although their most important function was motherhood, women needed to be educated about the "sublime" sexual activities, since "modesty[,] which is a delicacy, is often juxtaposed to priggishness[,] which is an artifice" (145) and which, ultimately, impedes family harmony. A woman's education must "mold her in such a way that she will prove to be the most pleasant of companions and never the most bothersome of appendages" (147). In addition, she must "go well instructed, well prepared for the struggle [to provide a livelihood]" (148) so as to legitimately aspire to carry out all manner of tasks that will offend neither her "delicateness" nor her physical qualities and that will allow her not to "live like [a] man, but to be at his level and not disadvantageously placed" (149).

Although in many respects Salvador Alvarado had a progressive outlook, he was, nevertheless, a man of his time, marked with certain beliefs about women. Hence, he never even questioned the precise role he had assumed for women. He did not seek a radical change as much as one benefiting both sexes and the state that had emerged from the

Revolution. His admiration for socialism may have exposed him to the discussions on women's issues among the Bolsheviks.

In 1917, the new Constitution was promulgated, purportedly expressing revolutionary and popular ideas. It did so only partially, however, since the progressive intentions, immersed in a hodgepodge of decrees and regulations, were lost. The Family Relations Law, enacted in April 1917, amended the 1884 Civil Code and introduced important changes regarding women.

On paper, the new Constitution gave women legal equality, with the same rights and duties as men, including the legal right to sign contracts and manage their own businesses and property. However, married women still needed their husband's permission to work, and they were still required to carry out domestic chores and care for their children. These requirements were later spelled out in the 1928 Civil Code. On this, Shirlene Soto (1990, 59) notes, "[h]ence . . . the sexual double standard was . . . institutionalized" within the legal system. Nevertheless, these discussions opened a space for debate on a range of topics.

Other benefits for women included legal equality with men to assume custody of their children and equal authority in the home, the elimination of the status of illegitimacy for children born out of wedlock, and the rights of concubines and mistresses. The norms also made it easier for both sexes to obtain a divorce by mutual consent, and divorce now dissolved the marriage bond. Grounds for divorce were now the same for women and men, except regarding adultery. Adultery by women was always grounds for divorce, whereas a woman had to show that her husband had committed adultery in the "conjugal house," that it caused scandal, or that he had insulted her. Thus, in practice the norms that had existed for centuries were maintained. Constitutional Article 123 regulated relations between workers and employers; established standards for the protection of women, especially pregnant women; and required equal pay for equal work.

Again, despite legal changes, the disparity between law and practice was maintained and the legal structure was filled with loopholes, frequently starting with the regulations themselves. Constitutional norms dealing with women were frequently ignored, since their specific oppression was not addressed in the laws passed to codify constitutional guarantees.

Although women nominally enjoyed legal equality, women's suffrage was not even discussed by the delegates who drafted the Constitution, although it had been proposed by some women, including Hermila Galindo. Still, some activists refused to be intimidated: although the Constitution did not give them the right to vote, it did grant them other civil rights, such as holding public office or sitting on commissions, meeting for political purposes, and petitioning. As a result, Hermila Galindo ran for legislative deputy in 1918. Although she claimed victory, it was never recognized.

The Years of Institutional Consolidation: The Struggle for Suffrage

Within the structure erected by the Revolution, women remained committed to overcoming the conditions that relegated them to an inferior status. Some women participated in issues that affected the nation's destiny with a high degree of awareness of their role, struggling to achieve the demands for legal equality proposed since the Revolution. In the early 1920s, feminist groups and leagues proliferated, were repressed, and continued to struggle defiantly. The work of Inés Malváez, Elena Torres, María Ríos Cárdenas, Luz Vera, Julia Nava de Ruisánchez, and Eulalia Guzmán stands out in this period.[5]

In 1922, the Mexican Feminist Council founded *La Mujer*, a magazine advocating stronger political rights and improved conditions for working women. That same year, a teacher, Elena Torres, and others represented the council in Baltimore at the first Pan-American Conference of Women, organized by American suffragists. Thus, the council joined the Pan-American League for the Improvement of Women, represented by Torres, a woman of radical ideas who had collaborated with Salvador Alvarado and Felipe Carrillo Puerto in Yucatán (Macías 1978, 294).

The Baltimore congress led to the 1923 Pan-American Feminist Congress for the Improvement of Women, attended by representatives from throughout Mexico. Conflicts soon arose, however, regarding leadership. The Yucatán delegation hoped to see a more radical agenda, and other differences arose among the feminists (ibid., 294–298).

A supporter of Alvarado, Felipe Carrillo Puerto, succeeded him as governor of Yucatán from 1922 to 1924. Carrillo Puerto shared his predecessor's ideas and tried to organize women, albeit based on his particular beliefs and ignoring the specific conditions of women in that time and place.

In 1922, Yucatán became the first state to give women "limited" voting rights. Rosa Torres won a popular election post, that of chair of the municipal council of Mérida, the state capital. In 1923 Carrillo Puerto's sister, Elvia, ran for state legislator, as did Beatriz Peniche, Raquel Dzib, and Guadalupe Lara (ibid., 290). That same year, Chiapas followed Yucatan's example, passing its own emancipatory measures for women.

Carrillo Puerto attempted to include women from every social class and group in his project. The feminist leagues in Mérida and throughout the state fought against drug addiction, alcoholism, and prostitution, and promoted literacy, hygiene, and birth control. These causes, as well as the leagues' support for free love and the right to divorce, annoyed Catholics and seriously hampered Carrillo Puerto's "measures to counter fanaticism" (*medidas desfanatizadoras*) (ibid., 336–338).

Josefina García, an active participant in the Rita Zetina Gutiérrez League, recalls that this "was precisely the era of organizing groups, and although it was true that among men this was difficult, [it was] much more so among women, since they had never had the slightest idea that they could aspire to be something beyond what their mothers had been, heads of household.... The idea was to awaken women's consciousness, to make them feel that they were persons" (Ortiz 1975, 14). In 1924, Carrillo Puerto was assassinated and his projects were shelved.

After Carrillo Puerto's death, the feminist movement became polarized, and achieving a consensus appeared unlikely. The 1925 Congreso de Mujeres de la Raza, organized by the League of Iberian and Hispanic American Women, was also beset by important differences of opinion. Some delegates stressed economic issues, while others emphasized legal or moral issues (Soto 1990, 106 ff). These divergences persisted for years to come.

During this period, women's rights' activists took part in national and international congresses, conferences, and meetings. The teachers' union was particularly forceful, even if teaching was considered an extension of traditional women's activities, these teachers were exceptionally involved and aware. They responded to the encouragement of José Vasconcelos, who became Minister of Public Education in 1921. Women teachers were highly regarded for their patience and abnegation.

Other Forms of Struggle . . . and of Inertia

Feminist organizations were not the only groups that women joined in order to carry forward their struggle. They also took part in broad-based movements unrelated to gender issues. In 1922, housewives as well as prostitutes participated in the tenant movement in Veracruz. Prostitutes were being forced to pay excessively high rents: if a simple house cost 80 pesos, the ramshackle rooms they lived in cost 150 (García Mundo 1976, 82). Hence, these residents of the "zone of fire," or red-light district (also known as the "horizontal ones"), were the first to declare a payment strike; their leadership in this struggle earned them the recognition of Hernán Proal, who, in a March 1922 speech, said:

> You deserve a vote of confidence from the strike committee
> and from all the inhabitants of Veracruz, because you were the

first to call the strike . . . you are true heroines for having laid
the first stone of this gigantic building that we have now constructed; you [were] the initiators and therefore deserve a very
warm hug of friendship. The Tenants' Red Union opens its arms
to you and calls you with all affection its beloved sisters. Yes,
gentlemen, and don't laugh [the word "sisters" had caused the
audience to laugh], these poor, despised women are not only our
companions but also our sisters, because [if we] analyze things,
[we will realize] that they, like us, are made of flesh and blood,
and there is no reason to exclude them from the brotherhood,
especially since they are fodder for the bourgeoisie's exploitation. (Ibid., 90)

Women from conservative sectors also took part in public life: women
had a proverbial role in the Cristero War (1926–1929), which engulfed the
Bajío region under the cry *"Viva Cristo Rey"* ("Long Live Christ the
King"). In this conflict, the *cristeros* defended the interests of the clergy
and opposed the secular policies of Plutarco Elías Calles. The influence
of Catholic women in education and customs became clear in the
coming years.

These were years of political experimentation throughout the nation.
The new governing elite were frequently the victims of crimes and
attacks. Laws were enforced with great difficulty and under pressure
from many sides. A strong state, under the guidance of a powerful
executive branch, was constructed. Women's attempt to establish greater
legal equality gradually succeeded. In 1928, President Calles cautiously
amended the Family Relations Law to increase equality through the civil
code. Some legal rights and capacities of women were enhanced; children born out of wedlock were recognized as legitimate; but women were
still not given suffrage and they continued to need their husband's
permission to work. Starting in the 1930s the laws were gradually
codified in regulations through which they were supposedly implemented and that remained in effect until the 1970s, when the reforms
promoted during International Women's Year were enacted.

Despite these changes, many traditional practices gradually returned
and regained their strength. People feared that with so much freedom
women might lose their femininity, meaning docility and submission,
thereby undermining the home. Nevertheless, the progress that had
been achieved and the specific needs of the new times meant that the
"interior-inferior" world would not return without a debate and that this
regression would not be achieved completely.

Some aspects of daily life remained static, such as the respect for
modesty and the staunch defense of marriage as the only option for

women. Starting in 1922, apparently to respond to and ward off the move toward emancipation taking place in the southeast, the newspaper *Excélsior* promoted the celebration of Mother's Day. This initiative was supported by merchants and became one of the most important rituals for Mexicans. "Queens for a day" received prizes based on the number of their children, the degree of their hardship, and the extent of their toil. The importance of abnegation and patience contrasted with the ideals being disseminated in Yucatán (Acevedo 1982).

Still, new ideas emerged. Aurelio de los Reyes (1993, 2:299) writes: "Undoubtedly, an agent for change in mentality and customs, particularly in women, was the cinema, which produced a series of dramatic social disruptions in their attitude toward life, their manner of dressing, of combing their hair." The 1920s were years of innovation, of short hair and short skirts, loose clothing, as compared with the long curls or braids, the corsets that clung to the figure and the enormous hats. Fashion was giving way to comfort. A svelte woman with an agile and athletic body could also feel beautiful. Music in variety and tent shows was lively and racy; Agustín Lara's songs were poetic and erotic; the *danzón* was sensual—couples "danced it in close unison and in a small square; floors were divided into squares and no one was to leave his or her square. I would dance *danzones* slowly, slowly, very slowly, paying attention" (Poniatowska 1984, 158). Postcards with photos of showgirls circulated from hand to hand; housewives kept their homes clean; and leftist intellectual women participated in the turbulent life of art and politics: women muralists and painters, and writers and critics of both sexes, questioned conventional norms with their brush or pen or in their speeches—and through their own lives. The militancy that had an effect was expressed more in women's lives than in conversations in barrooms. In this group, women such as Antonieta Rivas Mercado, Frida Kahlo, and Guadalupe Marín signified a complete renewal of norms and greater expectations from life, however far removed they were from the average woman.[6]

Cárdenas and the Frente Único Pro Derechos de la Mujer: A Slip 'Twixt the Cup and the Lip'

From 1928 to 1934—a period known as the *maximato*[7]—several important economic and political institutions were formed. One of these was the Partido Nacional Revolucionario (PNR), created in 1929 and later named the Partido de la Revolución Mexicana (PRM) and, finally, the Partido Revolucionario Institucional (PRI), by which it is still known today.

While the women's struggle remained strong in these years, a burning question was the degree to which the women's movement should be linked to the broader social struggle—a debate that had emerged in the 1920s and continued into the 1930s. Hence, two parallel congresses on prostitution held in 1934 dealt with the relationship between prostitution, poverty, and social inequality. Some delegates stressed the link between these factors, while others saw prostitution strictly as a moral issue.

Teachers, as members of the middle class, saw the possibility of linking the feminist cause to that of the popular classes, and held three National Congresses of Women Workers and Peasants (in 1931, 1933, and 1934), helping to establish the Children's Hospital and the Peasants' House. They also discussed problems specific to women, such as health conditions in factories and suffrage (Vidales 1980, 254). Elvia Carrillo Puerto and Florinda Lazos were instrumental in organizing the congresses.[8]

The overall quality of women's education had improved, but women were still a long way from better understanding their bodies and their sexuality. In 1932, the Mexican Eugenic Society reported to Secretary of Public Education Narciso Bassols its findings on the frequency of unwanted pregnancies and abortions among adolescents lacking a complete understanding of their actions. An attempt was made to ensure that the curricula make boys aware of their responsibilities and to educate girls on their bodies and in child-rearing (Britton 1976, 103). The National Parents' Union reacted immediately, claiming the initiative was part of a communist plot, defending the "innocence" of Mexican children, and encouraging students of both sexes to boycott their classes. In May 1934, Bassols was forced to resign. Modesty, understood as ignorance, continued to impede women's development and their awareness of their own abilities.

This climate permeated Lázaro Cárdenas's presidential term, from 1934 to 1940—a unique period, since the encouragement of grassroots organizations and the consolidation of the state brought important changes in national politics. Unions proliferated and grassroots organizations frequently turned into "national fronts," coordinating different currents of thought around specific objectives and giving the state the essential role of arbitrator.

In this form of organization, women's groups found an adequate venue for their demands. From 1935 to 1938 the Frente Único Pro Derechos de la Mujer (FUPDM; United Front for Women's Rights) was a national umbrella group for working-, middle-, and upper-class women from throughout the country, both literate and illiterate, Catholic and communist; its membership reached some 50,000 women organized in twenty-five sectors. Its first secretary general was Refugio García, and its most prominent members included Esther Chapa, Juana Belén Gutiérrez de Mendoza, Soledad Orozco, Adelina Zendejas, Frida Kahlo, and Concha Michel.

The Front's demands ranged from the general (opposition to imperialism, fascism, inflation) to those related directly to women and feminism. It called for a different role for women in education, in public life, in the workplace, and in land tenure, as well as more adequate social benefits and the extension of these benefits to indigenous women. Starting in 1937, the Front focused on the demand for the vote, considered the touchstone that would clear the way for other choices in life.

The Front was independent of the state, although it was supported by the PNR and the Communist Party (CP). Some women worked through other channels, such as Juana Belén Gutiérrez de Mendoza and Concha Michel, who belonged to Women's Republic, the name of which describes what the group hoped to establish. The theoretical underpinnings of this group were unusually clear for the times. For example, Concha Michel stated:

> The problem of women is not only class; with the working class, women have a common cause and a different cause.
> The common cause is that of most women who are exploited by the capitalists, the different cause is the reconquest of our autonomy regarding the social responsibility we have as mothers or as progenitors of the human species. (Esperanza Tuñón 1992, 115–116)

Michel, a Communist organizer of peasants and a folksinger, rejected the goal of absolute equality with men. She felt that women are not inferior—indeed, that men and women are equally strong and that they complement each other. She believed that socialism alone would not alleviate women's problems.

These visionaries attempted to create autonomous rural organizations to link women with the rural working class. They were a minority within the Front, and their positions soon contradicted the PNR/CP line. The Communist Party emphasized a broader struggle, believing that women's problems stemmed from social inequality. The PNR, by contrast, made women's issues a priority. Although Refugio García ascribed to the CP's position, she was respected by all. Despite these differences, the FUPDM clung to its belief that a social issue, such as women's rights, should be dealt with at the social level rather than individually or privately. This principle remains valid today.

In 1937 the different groups within the Front focused on their common goal—the demand for suffrage. Despite disenfranchisement, Refugio García and Soledad Orozco ran for deputy seats in Michoacán and Tabasco, but their evident victory was not acknowledged. Nevertheless, the women's struggle appeared to be making progress. In his third *Informe de Gobierno* (state of the union address), President Cárdenas spoke out clearly in favor of women's right to vote. Constitutional Articles 34 and 35, which in 1917 had remained unchanged with regard to the 1857 version, would have to be amended. The amendments were passed by both houses of Congress.

Women of the FUPDM now had only to wait for publication of the changes in the *Diario Oficial* (Official gazette). They congratulated each other and celebrated their victory. Inexplicably, however, the awaited amendments were never promulgated. Women would have to wait until 1953. At the express request of the First Magistrate of the Supreme Court, the Front joined the recently created Partido de la Revolución Mexicana in 1938, which superseded the Partido Nacional Revolucionario that Elías Calles had created in 1929.

Although Cárdenas had not granted women the right to vote, in 1939, convinced that justice dictated that they participate in politics as equals, he named Matilde Rodríguez Cabo head of the Department of Social Welfare for the Federal District and Esther Chapa director of the Assistance Committee for Spanish Children (that is, refugees from the Spanish Civil War).

Cárdenas's term was ending and the presidential succession was at a critical moment. On the eve of World War II, Mexico had taken pro-democracy stances both nationally and internationally. A conciliator, Manuel Ávila Camacho, was chosen to run on the PNR ticket. Perhaps fear that women voters would strengthen the most conservative sectors had stopped Cárdenas from granting women suffrage; we cannot be certain. However, suffrage continued to be a rallying cry for women, at a time when the women's struggle was increasingly being waged through official channels and institutions.

During the war, the FUPDM was renamed the Comité Coordinador de la Mujer para la Defensa de la Patria (Women's Coordinating Committee for the Defense of the Nation), and after the conflict ended it became the Bloque Nacional de Mujeres (National Women's Bloc), which would increasingly align itself with government policy.

6
From "Development" to Crisis
‰ ‱

In the 1940s, Mexico's economy expanded at a faster pace, its industry was strengthened, the middle class and cities grew; however, the price for this was the neglect of the countryside and an increasing dependence on wealthy countries. For women, this meant a greater role in production, although in the worst-paying jobs. Housewives began to acquire appliances. More women attended the university. Despite women's growing integration in society, the mass media and the traditional ideological machinery transmitted an outmoded portrayal of them that was inconsistent with the lives of women who worked and struggled and who had to become competitive and tenacious if they wanted to climb the social ladder. The divergence between the sublimation of myth and women's true, subordinate role was maintained: the cinema, radio, and popular music offered an archetype divorced from flesh-and-blood women.

The lyrics of the immensely popular poet and musician Agustín Lara provide eloquent representations of a certain view of women; for example, he described one "woman, divine woman" as having a "fascinating venomous gaze," and he praised her "alabaster quivering from a sonata of passion." Lara's portrayals, however, were far removed from the women torn between traditional obligations and those imposed by Mexico's capitalist growth.

The symbolism in Lara's songs is interesting because it places squarely in women "all the throbbing of a song, the dream of my existence"—regardless of their morality and pureness. He finds in prostitutes the incarnation of sex ("you know about the filters there are in love, you have the charm of lewdness").

Women were allowed to be sensual, as expressed by the rich voices of Ana María González and Toña "La Negra." This sensuality is projected, sublimated in the gender "like the blue shadow under a woman's eye" (María Teresa Lara). Their capacity to love gives them life, because

> . . . a woman who doesn't know how to love
> does not deserve to be called a woman

she's like a flower that doesn't give off its aroma
she's like wood that is unable to burn.

In Lara's boleros, to attain this passion, a woman must be

a dreamer, flirtatious and ardent
she must give herself up to love with frenzied
ardor . . .

and she needs a man who will know how to arouse her hidden abilities:

I lived asleep among shadows
without feeling the slightest emotion.
Once someone called me "sweetheart,"
my lethargy was broken.

Love was a recurring topic in songs, in movies, in radio serials, in the dreams that moved women, that motivated them, and that surely distracted more than one store clerk, factory worker, and family cook with fantasies of the life of a movie star with whom she had so little in common, such as María Félix, for example, who, with her dazzling statuesque beauty, jewelry, and self-assured, haughty manners, was even further removed from everyday women than were the Italian divas. As a consolation, these popular idols normally fared poorly in the movies, whereas fate rewarded good mothers (Sara García, for instance). American movies also transmitted their own moral and physical ideals: plump, shy, and passive beauty gave way to trim figures announcing diets, exercise, and an obsession with too many pounds. Women appeared to be more integrated in society, although they were also alienated in an obligatory lifestyle divorced from their own choices and possible fates.

As these images were being disseminated, the country was following a path from which women were not, in any event, divorced. The momentum toward women's suffrage continued. Miguel Alemán allowed women to vote in the 1947 municipal elections. In 1952, the Alliance of Mexican Women was formed and Amalia Caballero de Castillo León was named president. She paved the way for women's suffrage, which would finally be decreed by Adolfo Ruiz Cortines for the 1953 national elections. The decree giving women the right to vote was published in the *Diario Oficial* in October of that year.[1]

The state granted women the right to vote because a particular type of capitalist growth required legal equality among individuals, and, especially, because developed nations had already done so. Suffrage enhanced women's legal standing, although they were repeatedly told to be very careful in exercising this right so as to not lose their femininity or to forget their traditional roles as wives and mothers. The "eternal woman" continued to be the model for social morality. Women were given freedom, but it was a limited sort of freedom that ensured they would stay close to home.

Carlos Monsiváis (1993, 1) recalls the timidity with which women cast their ballots, "not as owners but as tenants of their recently acquired right." It seemed that women had not won the right to vote but that a state that needed to appear modern had granted it to them. Gabriela Cano (1995, 73) compares the two fundamental moments of the process: "If, for Lázaro Cárdenas, the establishment of women's suffrage was a question of democracy, for Adolfo Ruiz Cortines it was an act of chivalry." For Cárdenas, women's right to vote resulted from the equality of men and women, whereas for Ruiz Cortines it stemmed from women's worthiness, given their feminine, maternal characteristics and the consequent obligation to protect the nation, starting with the sanctity of the home.

In the economic sphere, from 1954 to 1968—the period known as the "Mexican Miracle"—the country implemented the import-substitution model. Gross domestic product rose 6 percent per year, outstripping population growth. The state, clearly centered around the presidency, was strong. Politically, society depended heavily on the state.

For three decades this model proved highly stable. By the 1970s, however, it entered into crisis, partially because of the burgeoning cities and the concomitant growth of the middle classes, who increasingly demanded a new political model. The 1968 student movement symbolized and portended the coming times. During the stability period, women had silently, but undeniably, taken part in public life; in the 1970s, they were unabashedly feminist.

Starting in 1982, the state's vulnerability as a promoter of growth became clear. The years since have further shown the bankruptcy of economic policy, and the outright political crisis appears to indicate that the models followed since the 1940s have run their course.

The state responded to the economic crisis by adopting neoliberal policies, including slashing government expenditure, privatizing state-owned companies, liberalizing foreign trade, and promoting exports. On January 1, 1994, Mexico, Canada, and the United States launched the North American Free Trade Agreement (NAFTA).

The gap between rich and poor has grown wider and the living standards of large sectors of the population have plummeted. Extreme poverty has increased: According to the Economic Commission on Latin America and the Caribbean (ECLAC), by 1981 the percentage of Mexicans living in poverty had fallen to 46 percent. However, by 1988, it had once again risen to 60 percent, similar to the 1977, pre–oil boom level.

To offset the social costs of economic policy, Carlos Salinas de Gortari (1988–1994) implemented the National Solidarity Program (PRONASOL). This public-works program proved insufficient, however. Women suffered from the "feminization of poverty," as they were the most affected by declining standards of living.

Mexican women have been present during the many changes seen in the last fifty years. To cite a few statistics:[2] In the 1990 census, just over half the country's 91 million inhabitants were women. The economic model encouraged women to have many children. In 1930, population growth was 1.7 percent; by 1960, it has risen to 3.4 percent. Between 1940 and 1980 the urban population increased elevenfold. The average number of children each woman bore declined from six in 1975 to four in 1985 and three by 1995. Birth control has been part of the government's policy since the 1970s, and it has been promoted in various ways, including through the slogan "A small family lives better." Women increasingly use birth control methods: in 1976, 30.2 percent of sexually active women used contraceptives; by 1987, 52.5 percent used them; and by 1995, 66.5 percent did.

The indigenous population, traditionally marginalized from economic progress and from mainstream life, has in recent years become a burning issue. In 1990, 10 percent of the overall population was indigenous; by 2000 this figure is expected to reach 20 percent. The 1994 indigenous uprising in Chiapas has underscored the need to attend these groups' needs, particularly those of indigenous women, some of whom, in fact, hold key leadership posts in the rebel ranks. *Zapatista* women have proposed a Revolutionary Law for Women demanding important changes in their communities, including the right to choose their husbands, to limit the number of children they bear, and to not be abused by their spouses.

In recent years, many social norms have been changed to apply equally to men and women. In 1974, Article 4 of the Constitution was amended to establish gender equality. Mexico had been designated the host of the First International Women's Conference, held by the United Nations in 1975, and the country's legislation clearly needed to be brought up-to-date. Likewise, the 1928 Civil Code was amended, providing services to working women and allowing peasant women to own land. In 1981, Mexico ratified the 1979 United Nations Convention on the Elimination of All Forms of Discrimination Against Women. The initial and persistent juridical inequality of women throughout our history has nearly been eliminated; however, the country's laws are frequently and easily overlooked. Inertia in mentalities strongly affects customs and habits.

The criminal code has also undergone positive changes. Courts have nearly ceased to consider "reputation and honor" a criterion for their rulings, although they continue to take it into account for accusations involving abortion and infanticide. Adultery is dealt with in the same way for men and women.

The state has created institutions to support women, especially CONAPO (National Population Council; 1974), which deals with problems related to women and families, and is still in existence today.

The percentage of women in the economically active population has risen considerably: from 7.3 percent in 1940 to 13.6 percent in 1950, 17.9 percent in 1960, 19.0 percent in 1970, 27.8 percent in 1980, and 32.0 percent in 1990. In addition, the type of women entering the labor force has also changed greatly, especially between 1970 and 1993. Before the 1982 crisis, young, single women and divorced, separated, or widowed women became wage earners. Since then, however, marriage has no longer been an obstacle to working, and the number of married mothers in the job market has increased. Ninety percent of the women who work outside the home also work in the home; that is, they have a double workday. Still, there are clearly regional differences.

The 1961 Federal Labor Law discriminated against women. In 1970 it was amended so that only pregnant women were excluded from working. Until 1974, a man could prevent his wife from working because of his legal obligation to support the family. Women were allowed to work only if it did not interfere with their obligations regarding home and children. Today most, but not all, states, have eliminated this restriction. Both the support for and custody of children are shared, although the responsibility for domestic chores continues to fall mostly on mothers and daughters.

Most working women are now employed in the textile, garment, food, and electronics industries. In recent years, however, they have increasingly found work in the informal economy or have joined the ranks of the underemployed. Statistics point to women's growing participation in the agricultural sector: from 9.2 percent in 1970 to 12.3 percent in 1990 and 14.2 percent in 1990. Still, censuses do not account for all facets of women's work, even in urban areas. For example, women who work in *maquiladoras* (assembly plants) or at home, generally sewing, are paid by the piece and lack social security (health insurance) or other minimum legal benefits. In agriculture, women's work is usually included in the work of the family unit. In addition, laws giving them the right to own parcels of land are probably not enforced. The agricultural crisis has forced women to migrate to the cities or to the northern border, where they work as maids, peddle wares, beg in the streets, or swell the ranks of the *maquiladora* work force.

Women are generally hired for subordinate positions: for each woman entrepreneur or business owner there are eight men. For the same or similar work, women receive lower salaries than men, but, in addition, they are placed in jobs with lower salaries. Sixty percent of working women lack social benefits. Whereas in the past women traditionally migrated to the cities to work as maids, in recent years they have increasingly headed north to work in *maquiladoras*. The United States also entices many women to leave home. Although the statistics are ambivalent, an estimated 57 percent of migrants are men, meaning 43 percent must be women.

Higher nationwide unemployment among men has forced more women to support their families and function as heads of household. This has led to a crisis in values, since mentalities shaped over centuries cannot automatically adjust to these changes.

That more Mexican women work in the public sector now than two generations ago has not necessarily improved their standard of living. Although work appears to be a necessary condition for their emancipation, having a job does not guarantee a desirable life.

Illiteracy has declined: Between 1970 and 1980, it fell from 25 percent to 17 percent of the population over the age of fifteen, and by 1990 to 12.7 percent. Nonetheless, the percentage of women among the illiterate population has risen from 58.6 percent in 1970 to 60.6 percent in 1980 and 62.5 percent in 1990. This predominance of women among the illiterate population is even more acute in rural areas.

Although access to higher education is nearly equal for women and men—with regional variations—this equality does not extend to all fields of study. Women are concentrated in what have traditionally been considered "women's" fields.

Health care has also deteriorated in recent years, although this deterioration has varied according to region and class. Problems related to abortion are considerable. Since abortion is a crime, exact numbers are hard to come by, but abortion is believed to be the fifth leading cause of death among women. Most women who undergo abortions are Catholics and already have children. Only 3.5 percent of abortions are legal (the practice is legal when the pregnancy threatens the mother's life or is the product of a rape). Still, the topic is strongly debated today.

AIDS was first detected in Mexico in 1983. The percentage of AIDS patients who are women rose from 6.9 percent in 1985 to 16.2 percent in 1990. In 1994, 13.6 percent of registered AIDS patients were women. The first cause of AIDS infections in women is heterosexual intercourse, followed by blood transfusions.

Women's roles in politics have varied from sector to sector. In formal political channels, their participation has been minimal. In 1982, Rosario

Ibarra de Piedra ran on the ticket of the Revolutionary Workers Party
(PRT), as did Cecilia Soto for the Workers Party (PT) in 1994. In 1976,
Rosa Luz Alegría became the first woman cabinet member, as minister
of tourism. Through 1997 only five women had held cabinet-level
positions.[3] In 1979, Griselda Álvarez became the first state governor (in
Colima), followed by Beatriz Paredes in Tlaxcala in 1986. Of the 628
seats in the Chamber of Deputies and the Senate for the 1995–1998
legislative term, only 13.7 percent were held by women, and only 2.8
percent of the country's mayors were women. Discussion within parties
(mainly the Party of the Democratic Revolution, or PRD, and the
Institutional Revolutionary Party, or PRI) currently centers on quotas
for women. Women's advocates have asked that this minimum be set at
30 percent. The left-leaning PRD has established this quota in its bylaws,
although it has not yet carried it out.

Unlike some countries, Mexico does not have a federal cabinet post
for women's affairs. On the state level, only Guerrero has established
one. In the mid-1990s, this was one topic regarding women being
discussed in government. In 1990, Dulce María Sauri was named coor-
dinator of the National Women's Program, which is directed by the
Ministry of Interior (Gobernación).

If in official party politics women have had a minimal role, in other
areas their presence has been much more prominent. We must distinguish between broad-based women's movements and feminist movements per se. Women in popular organizations have worked to solve
their everyday problems, many related to public services. They have also
done so in working-class neighborhoods, where, for example, the National Coordinating Committee of the independent Urban Popular
Movement (CONAMUP) has played an important role. The Benita
Galeana Coordinating Committee has also brought together urban
popular-class women. And the government-sponsored PRONASOL's
Women in Solidarity section worked to improve women's daily lives.

Feminism has made considerable strides in the last twenty-five years.
In 1964 the National Women's Union sponsored a Congress for the
Unification of Mexican Women, which made labor and political demands, although its struggle was not specifically of and for women.
Starting with the 1968 student movement, several issues were raised
that did not become formal demands until the 1970s. The influence of
U.S. and European feminists during this period is clear. Most women
who joined this struggle were left-leaning, middle-class university
students. They gradually succeeded in reaching out to workers and
peasants.

A September 1970 article by Marta Acevedo, published in the magazine *Siempre*, raised awareness regarding many issues. Titled "Nuestro

sueño está en escarpado lugar" (Our struggle is in a steep place), it detailed demands made by women in San Francisco, California, in commemoration of the fiftieth anniversary of women's suffrage in the United States. Topics such as the double workday, discrimination in the work place, women's portrayal by the mass media, the decriminalization of abortion and the need for it to be legal and free, violence against women, and rape began to be discussed. In sum, the inequality women suffered in their everyday lives was stressed.

On May 10, 1971—Mother's Day—the group Mujeres en Acción Solidaria (MAS) staged a protest at Mexico City's Monument to Mothers. On the same day, candidates in the Miss Mexico contest took part in a televised event there. The contrast was enormous, and the empowerment women received from the event was essential for their struggle.

In 1972, the Image and Reality of Women in Mexico colloquium was held,[4] at which many issues that concerned feminists were brought up. Women's organizations subsequently began to proliferate: the Women's Liberation Movement and the National Women's Movement, both with links to the mass media; the Women's Front Countercongress to the World Women's Conference (1975); The Revolt Collective, which published a newspaper and was given a page in the *unomásuno* newspaper; the Mexican Feminist Movement; the Coalition of Women Feminists, which published the magazine *Cíhuatl; Lesbos*, a group of homosexual women; and Feminist Struggle. In addition, the magazine *FEM* was founded, which continues to disseminate positions and information for and by women today.

The 1970s also saw the formation of associations. In 1976, the Coalition of Feminist Women—formed by the Mexican Feminist Movement, the Women's Liberation Movement, and the National Women's Movement—called for "voluntary motherhood," that is, for legal, free abortion, and it continued to speak out against violence and rape. In 1979, the National Front of Struggle for Women's Freedom and Rights (FNALIDM) attempted to bring together the efforts of these different organizations. It submitted to the Chamber of Deputies a bill on voluntary motherhood. Although the proposal was not acted upon, it underscored the concerns of an era and encouraged many women, and men, to join the struggle.

The trend continued in the eighties and nineties. The Coordinating Committee for Autonomous Feminist Groups was founded in 1982, the National Women's Network in 1983, and the National Front of Struggle for Voluntary Motherhood in 1991.

Although women's organizations had a wide range of concerns, violence was among the most prominent, undoubtedly because many Mexican women continued to be the victims of violence, supposedly as a result of men's "consubstantial" violence. In 1979, the Center to Support Raped Women (CAMVAC) was founded, and in 1980 the Autonomous Group of University Women (GAMU) expressed its concern regarding violence. In 1983 a group of women senators unsuccessfully sought passage of a bill to outlaw sexual harassment. Starting in 1984, the Collective for Struggle against Violence toward Women (COVAC) offered medical, legal, and psychological support to victims of violence.

The emphasis on this issue produced results: In 1989 the first Office Specializing in Sex Crimes was created and by 1994 there were sixteen such offices. The Mexico City attorney general's office opened family-violence centers. In April 1996, the Mexico City Assembly of Representatives passed the Intrafamily Assistance and Violence Prevention Law. In November of that year, an international forum was held on the topic. The debate regarding violence against woman in the 1990s has been intense.

Discussion on rape has also been passionate, although the topic has clearly not been accorded the importance it merits. Abortion has also gained attention. In 1990, Chiapas legislators submitted a bill to decriminalize the procedure. Although the initiative did not pass, it exposed broader sectors of the population to the issue.

Organizing has been carried out in other ways, sometimes at the party level, sometimes through other channels, as for example, through the Comité de Presos, Perseguidos, Exiliados y Desaparecidos Políticos (Committee for Prisoners, Persecuted Persons, Exiles, and Those Disappeared for Political Reasons), created in 1978, most of whose members are mothers of victims. In the mid-nineties, Rosario Ibarra de la Piedra was the indisputable leader of the committee.

Participation in independent unions has been important, particularly in the September 19 National Seamstresses Union, made up of women garment workers affected by the 1985 earthquakes. The union has exposed many problems in the garment industry, including ten-hour workdays in sweatshops that fail to pay even the minimum wage.

Since 1988, in addition to economic and social demands, women have made demands concerning democracy, justice, and the respect for elections. Women in the Struggle for Democracy is an umbrella group of different movements and organizations. To a large degree, the concern with democracy stems from the strongly contested 1988 presidential election awarded to Carlos Salinas de Gortari. Fifty-six percent of the voters in that election were women.

In 1991, the National Convention of Women for Democracy was created. It nominated activists committed to women's rights, to the decriminalization of abortion, and to the struggle against violence as candidates for the Chamber of Deputies. On October 5, 1996, the Women's National Assembly was formed, with the participation of twenty-seven organizations that hoped to ensure a more effective participation of women in politics and to see that the recently established National Women's Program would outlast the current presidential term and be given sufficient resources. The Assembly also advocated several broad political reforms intended to encourage the consolidation of democracy.

Today groups are making a wide range of gender-based demands. They are organized in fronts, in coordinating committees, in nongovernmental organizations—many of the latter with international funding—and in grassroots groups, among others. Their members include militants, residents of popular neighborhoods, women concerned with civic participation and democracy, and even "sex workers" who have organized for their own protection and defense. In academia, interest has also increased, as many universities and other higher-education centers have included women's issues in their courses of study.

Since 1987, the newspaper *La Jornada* has published the supplement *Doble Jornada* (Double workday), and the magazine *Debate Feminista* has run articles on a high theoretical level. Women's magazines are also published outside the capital, including *La Ventana* in Guadalajara and *Gen-eros* in Colima. Some radio stations have also aired programs with a women's perspective.

We can now speak of a broad-based women's movement in which workers, grassroots groups, and feminists participate. Still, whereas the emphasis was once on human equality and the aspiration to social equality, today differences between individuals are more closely observed and fairness is stressed. The struggle has been waged on many fronts, and influence has gradually been exerted on reluctant public decision makers.

And although Mexican women enjoy considerable legal equality, changes in informal education (customs, the media, the church, among others) and in men's and even women's attitudes have not kept pace with women's achievements. Bringing about such a change would give all Mexicans—women and men—a better life. Gender relationships continue to be hierarchical and asymmetrical. Social contradictions have affected the social network and they impede women's proper development. De jure equality is not de facto equality; although the former is a necessary condition for the latter, women's oppression is more complex and is rooted in issues outside the legal sphere.

Conclusion
The Temptation to Exist
⥰⥼

Mexico's history has been long and painful; its people have had to insert themselves into the global system, with all that this entails: birth, death, change, adaptation, and continuity. Integration has meant trying to catch up with and jump onto a moving car, with the resulting detrimental consequences for the country's own well-being. This happened to Mexico when it tried to climb onto the moving car of Christian culture, of capitalism, of the European patriarchal system, of the liberalism that declared "we are all equals," even as inequality was clear. Still, integration into that global system, which unilaterally established its own rules and values, has also entailed a process of internal integration—prior or simultaneous, but always partial—required for a minimal degree of understanding of the world.

Mexican women have been present and have participated in this process; at times they have even been the specific instrument of it. In the case of *mestizaje*, Malinche is not a gratuitous symbol but the expression of a reality. For that reason she is as hated as Guadalupe is venerated.

Although women have belonged and have been committed to their respective social classes, as a gender they have also had to endure a patriarchal order that translates sexual difference into inferiority.

Race was important at the beginning of the colonial period, when the association between indigenous and vanquished was more evident than was the importance of money and the creation of a large class of mestizos and *castas*. In the seventeenth century, Sor Juana Inés de la Cruz, a criolla, symbolized the repression against women. Being a person of exceptional abilities, she faced multiple obstacles in pursuing her intellectual vocation, since social morality called for a strictly domestic role for women, who were taught to value submission, dedication, instinct, and inertia. On the basis of social class, more than race, women performed similar roles, and they resisted these roles and participated in history as best they could.

The development of capitalism further complicated women's standing by bringing about a situation that was both unjust and contradictory. The system required an ideological underpinning: the equality of individual, inalienable opportunities that led each person, in accordance with his or her talent, to fulfill his or her own goals. Women were incorporated into this dynamic even though evident contradictions remained unresolved. At work, in public life, and in politics they were theoretically offered equal civil and legal rights and the same opportunity to obtain an education. None of this, however, solved the oppression exercised against them because of their gender and that went beyond the purview of the workplace and the political and educational institutions.

Today women work outside the home, but they must do so without violating their nature—supposedly antithetical to profits—and without the desire for power or the ability to compete. They have civil and political rights, but they must be careful not to violate patriarchal models!—models that have been determined by a system of male privilege and that have been instilled in them as well. Given the supposed equality of rights, women must struggle to make these rights applicable to them; given their sexual condition, they must attempt to construct a hierarchy alongside the male hierarchy.

The passage of a greater number of egalitarian laws is not sufficient; laws must truly benefit women. More than merely becoming incorporated into the workplace, women must ensure that work will entail liberation and not a double burden. Change will require other strategies because women's oppression also exists in ideology, in an ideology that contains both old and new underlying elements that inform people from different social classes and with varying levels of education.

Today, newsstands are filled with women's magazines that represent transnational corporations and their ideology and that allow women's sexuality, just as they once targeted men's sexuality. The emphasis now, however, is on pleasure rather than motherhood. "Efficiency," then, becomes the reason for exercising an eroticism that, once again, is imposed from without, not based on women's own bodies and their own desires. According to the message transmitted by magazines, this capacity is coupled with professional success (which means earning much money) and with handling household chores in an efficient, modern way. Messages are recycled with the "liberation" label, although the essential contents are not affected.

A glance at women's participation in Mexico shows that we are far from the finish line, that there is much work to be done. Sexism is neither a conspiracy of one sex against the other nor a biological fact. It is a social system. Faced with this system, women have collectively become aware that they deserve the best possible world and that this world is worth struggling for.

History can contribute to this: it can kindle our memory, offer a looking-glass rather than a mirage, return us to past dreams and realities that will help women overcome silence. Only the existence of a past can allow us to aspire toward a future. To work for change, we must delve into history, which is another way of delving into life.

Notes

✠✠

1. Women in the Mexica World

1. "Aridamerica" refers to an arid area in northern Mesoamerica, the majority of whose inhabitants were nomadic.

2. See also Enriqueta Tuñón Pablos (1991).

3. Fifth Sun (Quinto Sol) refers to the Mexica belief that time was clearly demarcated into periods; when one age ended, so did the world, and it was then re-created by the gods, with new humans and other forms of life.

4. *Calpulli* consisted of groups of families who were joined in kinship or friendship and who shared a piece of land that they farmed. They considered themselves to be descendants of common ancestors whom they venerated.

5. "And when you speak, do not hasten to speak; [rather, do so] not with uneasiness, but little by little and calmly; when you speak, you shall not raise your voice nor will you speak very softly, but [rather] with a medium pitch; you shall not raise the pitch of your voice very much when you speak or when you greet [others], nor will you speak through your nostrils; but [rather], may your word be modest and have a good sound, and [may] the pitch of your voice [be] medium; do not be peculiar in your words" (Sahagún 1956, vol. 2, bk. 6, Ch. 9, 132–133).

6. Be sure, daughter, that in your walk your are modest; do not walk with haste or with very long strides because it is a sign of pomp to walk slowly, and walking hurriedly [expresses] uneasiness and unsettledness . . . when it is necessary to jump over a stream, you will jump modestly, so that you appear neither heavy and clumsy nor light . . . do not carry your head very inclined or your body very stooped over, nor walk with your head very high or very raised, because this is a sign of a poor upbringing . . . do not cover your mouth, nor [let] your face [show] shame . . . do not go looking here nor there, nor turning your head to look at one place or another; neither will you go looking at the heaven, nor will you go looking at the ground . . . look at everyone with a serene countenance. In doing this you will give no one the occasion to become angry at you" (ibid.).

7. "Show your face and disposition as you should, and in the manner which is suitable, so that you will not go about with a countenance that is either angry or smiling" (ibid.).

8. "Be sure also, daughter, not to give anything for the words you hear [while] you go along the path, nor imagine them, regardless of what those who go or come might say; be careful not to respond or to speak; rather, do as if you

didn't hear or understand, in this manner, no one will be able to say, verily, [that] you said such a thing" (ibid.).

9. A *huipil* is a loose knee- or ankle-length dress with openings for the arms and neck. It may be worn above or below a *cueitl*, or wrap-around skirt . *Nahuas* are skirts. Footwear consists of *cactli* or *huaraches* (sandals made of interwoven leather), and rebozos (shawls) or *quechquémetl* (a triangular-shaped cloth used by women to cover their breasts) are used to keep warm. In the countryside, women did not have to cover their breasts.

10. "Hence infamy and disgrace will occur to our ancestors and men and senators from which we come, from which you were born, and you will sully their illustrious fame and their glory with the filth and dirt of your sin" (Sahagún 1956, vol. 2, bk. 6, ch. 18, 135).

11. "Our lord is merciful; however, if you betray your husband, even if it is not known, even if it is not made public, God, who is everywhere, will take revenge for your sin, such that you will never have content or rest [or] a peaceful life, and he will make your husband always be angry at you and always speak to you with anger" (ibid.).

12. The document describing this, contained in Fernando de Alva Ixtlixóchitl's *Obras históricas,* is reproduced in a book by Enriqueta Tuñón Pablos (1991, 122–125).

13. See also Serge Gruzinski (1979, 129–142).

2. Women in New Spain

1. The *encomienda* was an arrangement by which Spaniards were permitted to be the guardians of Indians, who were considered minors. Hence, in exchange for educating and caring for the Indians, Spaniards exercised usufruct over the tribute paid by them. The *encomienda,* in theory, did not allow either the seizing of Indian land or the enslavement of its inhabitants, but in practice Indian lands often were, in fact, taken and their inhabitants enslaved.

2. Regarding the Pueblo Indians, see Ramón Gutiérrez (1991).

3. *Mestizos* refers to the offspring of Spaniards and Indians, usually from a union in which the man was Spanish and the woman Indian. *Castas* are the offspring of various groups, including blacks, Indians, and whites, regardless of the preponderance of any of these groups.

4. The Indians called Cortés by this name.

5. See Bolívar Echeverría (1994, 129–138).

6. Regarding Isabel Moctezuma, see Donald Chipman (1987, 253–262).

7. See also Seminario de Historia de las Mentalidades (1985b), and Sergio Ortega (1985).

8. According to Solange Alberro, women were rarely brought before the Inquisition Tribunal, and those who *were* tried were charged with crimes relating to witchcraft and erotic magic (quoted in Ramos Escandón 1987, 88–89). Also see Solange Alberro (1989, 27–89) and Ruth Behar (1989).

9. The *maja* wore a brightly colored dress with flounces; the *lagarterana,* or native of the region of Toledo, wore an embroidered dress with sequins. The *charro* suit was characterized by a tight, embroidered vest and pants with silver-colored trim and buttons.

10. An *amiga* was a teacher without formal training who taught basic

reading and writing at home.

11. See Ana María Atondo (1985) and Alfredo López Austin (1982).

12. The royal warrant is reproduced in Josefina Muriel (1974, 34).

13. According to an inspector named Tello de Sandoval (Muriel 1982, 36).

14. For more bibliographic information, see Muriel (1992, 97–104).

15. Jean Franco (1989) analyzes the cases of María de Jesús Tomelín (sixteenth and seventeenth centuries) and of María de San Joseph (seventeenth and eighteenth centuries).

16. For example: "I study not to write and much less to teach, which in me would be excessive haughtiness, but only to see if by studying I will be less ignorant" (de la Cruz [1690] 1929, 12).

17. A *chamizo* was the son of a mestizo man and a *castiza* (mixed Spanish and mestizo); a *saltapatrás* was the offspring of a *chino* and an *india;* a *lobo* was the product of a marriage between a *saltapatrás* and a *mulata;* a *coyote* was the son of a mestizo and an *india; tente-en-el-aire* referred to the offspring of a Spaniard and a *tornatrás* (in turn, the product of a union between a Spaniard and an *albina); albarrasado* was used in reference to the child of a *lobo* and an *india;* and *zambo* was the son of a black man and an Indian woman.

18. The full name was "Real Cédula sobre Enajenación de Bienes Raíces y Cobro de Capitales de Capellanía y Obras Pías para la Consolidación de Vales Reales" (Royal warrant concerning the transfer of property and collection of chaplaincy and charitable funds for the consolidation of the royal fund).

19. The marquis de Condorcet's name was Jean Antoine-Nicolas de Caritat. He wrote *Sketch for a Historical Picture of the Progress of the Human Mind* (1795), a fundamental text for the French Revolution. He advocated civil and educational equality for women.

20. Her speech was titled "Necesidad de un establecimiento de educación para los jóvenes mexicanos" (The need to establish education for Mexican youth; Gonzalbo 1985, 150).

3. Mexican Women in the Nineteenth Century

1. The Freemason lodges grouped together the incipient political organizations during the nation's early years. Roughly speaking, the Scottish Freemasons wanted to keep their class privileges, while the Yorks proposed reforms.

2. See Manuel Dublán and José Manuel Lozano (1878).

3. See the introduction to Guelberdi's document in Julia Tuñón (1991, 3:73–74).

4. As was made evident in the documentation in Federico Solórzano's personal archive, in Guadalajara, Jalisco.

5. For example: *Presente Amistoso Dedicado a las Señoritas Mexicanas* (Friendly present dedicated to Mexican señoritas), *La Semana de las Señoritas,* (Weekly for señoritas); *Revista Científica y Literaria de México* (Scientific and literary review of Mexico), *Semanario de las Señoritas Mejicanas* (Weekly of Mexican señoritas), *El Monitor Republicano* (The republican monitor). See also Manuel Payno (1984) and Francisco Zarco (1968).

6. Melchor Ocampo was one of the most important thinkers of the Reforma.

7. Also see Julia Tuñón (1991, 44–45).

8. Josefina Muriel shows that, by 1800, convents had lost their protective function (1974, 116, 117–119).

9. Dublán and Lozano, 1878, 9: 32 (Feb. 2) and 9: 128 (March 27), respectively.

10. Ibid., 594–595.

11. Ibid., 599.

4. Peace in Porfirian Times

1. Ricardo Flores Magón was an early-twentieth-century social activist; he at first espoused liberal ideas, but he later embraced anarchism.

2. See, for example, Soledad González Montes and Pilar Iracheta (1987).

3. The basic text on this topic is Lara and Pardo (1901). Contemporary studies include Suárez and Ríos (1992, 4–9); Núñez (1996); and Sagredo (1996).

4. See Chapter 5, note 7.

5. The complete title was *La Mujer Mexicana: Revista Mensual Científico Literaria Consagrada a la Evolución, Progreso y Perfeccionamiento de la Mujer.* It dealt with "women's evolution, progress, and perfectioning."

6. Also see Lau and Ramos (1993, 24–28); INEHRM (1992).

7. See the program of the Hijas de Anáhuac in CEHSMO (1975, 19).

5. From Revolution to Stability

1. Quoted in Turner (1967, 606–607).

2. See *La mujer en la resistencia contra el invasor* (INAH, 1985).

3. See document cited in *Historia Obrera* (1975, 21).

4. Cited in de los Reyes (1973, 1:199).

5. Anna Macías (1978, 286–301); also see Ana Lau (1987) and Shirlene Soto (1990).

6. On this point, see Jean Franco (1989, 102–123, chapter 5). Among other texts, also see Bartra (1994); Bradu (1991); del Conde (1976); Herrera (1983); Malvido (1995); Schneider (1987); Tibol (1977); and Zamora (1987).

7. So called because General Plutarco Elías Calles, after leaving office, held a tight rein over the governments of presidents Emilio Portes Gil, Abelardo Rodríguez, and Pascual Ortiz Rubio, and was thus called the *Jefe Máximo* (Supreme Chief).

8. See respective documents in *Historia Obrera* (1975, 24–44).

6. From "Development" to Crisis

1. See Enriqueta Tuñón (1987, 181–89).

2. The following data are, for the most part, based on information from Instituto de la Mujer-FLACSO (1993), INEGI-UNIFEM (1995), Esperanza Tuñón (1997).

3. The others are María de los Ángeles Moreno, who was minister of fishing; María Elena Vázquez Nava, who headed the comptrollership; and Silvia Hernández, who held the post of minister of tourism. Julia Carabias is the minister of the environment as this book goes to press (1998).

4. See Elena Urrutia (1979).

References

⊱⊰

The following abbreviations are used in the references:

CEESTEM—Centro de Estudios Económicos y Sociales del Tercer Mundo
CEHSMO—Centro de Estudios Históricos del Movimiento Obrero Mexicano
CIESAS—Centro de Investigaciones y Estudios Superiores de Antropología Social
CONACULTA—Consejo Nacional para la Cultura y las Artes
CONAPO—Consejo Nacional de Población
CONDUMEX—Nacional de Conductores Eléctricos
DEH—Dirección de Estudios Históricos
FFyL—Facultad de Filosofía y Letras (UNAM)
IIA—Instituto de Investigaciones Antropológicas (UNAM)
IIE—Instituto de Investigaciones Estéticas (UNAM)
IIH—Instituto de Investigaciones Históricas (UNAM)
IIJ—Instituto de Investigaciones Jurídicas (UNAM)
IIS—Instituto de Investigaciones Sociales (UNAM)
INAH—Instituto Nacional de Antropología e Historia
INEGI—Instituto Nacional de Estadística, Geografía e Informática
INEHRM—Instituto Nacional de Estudios Históricos de la Revolución Mexicana
INFONAVIT—Instituto del Fondo Nacional de la Vivienda para los Trabajadores
INPI—Instituto Nacional de Protección a la Infancia
PUEG—Programa Universitario de Estudios de Género (UNAM)
SEP—Secretaría de Educación Pública
SPP—Secretaría de Programación y Presupuesto
UAM—Universidad Autónoma Metropolitana
UNAM—Universidad Nacional Autónoma de México
UNIFEM—United Nations Development Fund for Women

Acevedo, Marta. 1970. "Nuestro sueño está en escarpado lugar: Crónica de un miércoles santo entre las mujeres. (Women´s Liberation San Francisco)." *La cultura en México.* Suplemento de *Siempre* 901 (September 30): ii–vi.
———. 1971. *Ni diosa ni mártir: La mujer de hoy en la lucha por su liberación.* Colección Los Muros Tienen la Palabra. Mexico City: Extemporáneos.
———. 1982. *El diez de mayo.* Imágenes de México 7. Mexico City: SEP/Cultura, Memoria y Olvido.

Alberro, Solange. 1988. *Inquisición y sociedad en México: 1571–1700.* Mexico City: Fondo de Cultura Económica, Sección de Obras de Historia.

———. 1989. "Templando destemplanzas: Hechiceras veracruzanas ante el Santo Oficio de la Inquisición, Siglos XVI–XVII." In *Del dicho al hecho . . . Transgresiones y pautas culturales en la Nueva España.* Seminario de Historia de las Mentalidades. Colección Científica. Mexico City: INAH.

Alberro, Solange, et al. 1980. "El discurso inquisitorial sobre los delitos de bigamia, poligamia y de solicitación." In *Seis ensayos sobre el discurso colonial relativo a la comunidad doméstica,* pp. 215–231. Cuaderno de Trabajo 35. Mexico City: DEH-INAH.

———. 1987. "Herejes, brujas y beatas: Mujeres ante el tribunal del Santo Oficio de la Inquisición en la Nueva España." In *Presencia y transparencia: La mujer en la historia de México,* ed. Carmen Ramos Escandón. Mexico City: El Colegio de México.

Alegría, Juana Armanda. 1974. *Psicología de las mexicanas.* Mexico City: Editorial Samo.

Alonso, José Antonio. 1981. *Sexo, trabajo y marginalidad urbana.* Estudios Sociales. Mexico City: Edicol.

Altamirano, Ignacio Manuel. 1966. *Clemencia.* Colección de Escritores Mexicanos 3. Mexico City: Editorial Porrúa.

Alvarado, Salvador. 1976. *Antología Ideológica.* Colección SEP/Setentas 305. Mexico City: SEP.

Álvarez, Alfredo Juan. 1979. *La mujer joven en México.* Mexico City: El Caballito.

Año internacional de la mujer. 1975. Programa de México. June–July. Documents.

Aranda, Clara Eugenia, Teresa Arreola, Jorge Carrión, Margarita de Leonardo y Elaine Levine. 1975. *La mujer: Explotación, lucha, liberación.* Colección SEP/Setentas 182. Mexico City: SEP.

Arizpe, Lourdes. 1975. *Indígenas en la Ciudad de México: El caso de las "Marías."* Colección SEP/Setentas 182. Mexico City: SEP.

Arrom, Silvia Marina. 1976. *La mujer mexicana ante el divorcio eclesiástico: 1800–1857.* Colección SEP/Setentas 251. Mexico City: SEP.

———. 1981. "Cambios en la condición jurídica de la mujer mexicana en el siglo XIX." In *Memoria del Segundo Congreso de Historia del Derecho Mexicano (1980),* coordinated by José Luis Soberanes. Estudios Históricos 10. Mexico City: UNAM-IIJ.

———. 1985a. "Changes in Mexican Family Law in the Nineteenth Century: The Civil Codes of 1870 and 1884." *Journal of Family History* 10 (3): 305–317.

———. 1985b. *The Women of Mexico City, 1790–1857.* Stanford: Stanford University Press.

Arróniz, Marcos. 1991. *Manual del viajero en México o Compendio de la historia de la ciudad de México.* Mexico City: Instituto José María Luis Mora. Facsimile.

Atondo, Ana María. 1982. "Prostitutas, alcahuetes y mancebas. Siglo XVI." In *Familia y sexualidad en la Nueva España. Memoria del Primer Simposio de Historia de las Mentalidades: Familia, Matrimonio y Sexualidad en la Nueva*

España. Colección SEP/Ochentas 41. Mexico City: Fondo de Cultura Económica-SEP.

———. 1985. "La memoria en el discurso de la fornicación. Siglo XVI." In *La memoria·y el olvido. Segundo Simposio de Historia de las Mentalidades.* Colección Científica 144. Mexico City: INAH-SEP.

———. 1992. *El amor venal y la condición femenina en el México colonial.* Colección Divulgación. Mexico City: INAH.

Ávila Camacho, Manuel. 1941. *Mensaje a las madres mexicanas.* Mexico City: Secretaría de Gobernación.

Balbuena, Bernardo de. 1974. *Grandeza mexicana.* Mexico City: Departamento del Distrito Federal, Secretaría de Obras y Servicios. Colección Popular, Ciudad de México 20.

Barbieri, Teresita de. 1980. *Mujer y vida cotidiana.* Mexico City: SEP. Colección SEP/Ochentas 60.

Bartra, Eli. 1994. *Frida Kahlo: Mujer, ideología y arte.* Barcelona: Icaria.

Basurto, Jorge. 1993. *Vivencias femeninas de la Revolución.* Colección Testimonios. Mexico City: INEHRM–Secretaría de Gobernación.

Batalla, Clementina Bassols de. 1960. *La mujer en la Revolución mexicana.* Mexico City: N.p.

Behar, Ruth. 1989. "Brujería sexual, colonialismo y poderes femeninos: Opiniones del Santo Oficio de la Inquisición en México." In *Sexualidad y matrimonio en la América hispánica,* ed. Asunción Lavrin. Colección Los Noventa. Mexico City: CONACULTA-Grijalbo.

Bergon, Frank, ed. 1979. *The Western Writings of Stephen Crane.* A Signet Classic. New American Library. New York: Times Mirror.

Bermúdez, María Teresa. 1988. "Las leyes, los libros de texto y la lectura, 1857–1876." In *Historia de la lectura en México.* Seminario de Historia de la Educación. Mexico City: Ediciones del Ermitaño–El Colegio de México.

Blanco, Iris. 1990. "El sexo y su condicionamiento cultural en el mundo prehispánico." In *Between Borders: Essays on Mexicana/Chicana History,* ed. Adelaida R. del Castillo. La Mujer Latina Series. Encino, Calif.: Floricanto Press.

Bradu, Fabianne. 1991. *Antonieta, 1900–1931.* Mexico City: Fondo de Cultura Económica.

Bremauntz, Alberto. 1937. *El sufragio femenino desde el punto de vista constitucional.* Mexico City: Frente Socialista de Abogados.

Britton, John A. 1976. *Educación y radicalismo en México 1: Los años de Bassols.* Colección SEP/Setentas 287. Mexico City: SEP.

Calderón de la Barca, Frances Erskine Inglis de. 1970. *Life in Mexico: The Letters of Fanny Calderón de la Barca with New Material from the Author's Private Journals.* Edited and annotated by Howard T. Fisher and Marion Hall Fisher. New York: Anchor Books.

Calvo, Vicente. 1843. *Descripción del Departamento de Sonora, 1843.* N.p.

Cano, Gabriela. 1995. "Una ciudadanía igualitaria: El presidente Lázaro Cárdenas y el sufragio femenino." In *Desdeldiez* (December). Mexico City: Centro de Estudios de la Revolución Mexicana Lázaro Cárdenas, Asociación Civil.

Cano, Gabriela, and Verena Radkau. 1989. *Ganando espacios. Historias de vida:*

Guadalupe Zúñiga, A lura Flores y Josefina Vicens. Colección Correspondencia. Mexico City: UAM-Iztapalapa.

Cano Gabriela, Carmen Ramos, and Julia Tuñón. 1991. *Ensayos: Problemas en torno a la historia de las mujeres.* Cuaderno 55. Mexico City: UAM-Iztapalapa.

Carranza, Venustiano. 1917. *Ley sobre relaciones familiares.* Mexico City: Imprenta de Gobernación.

Carrera Stampa, Manuel. 1961. "Heroínas de la guerra de independencia." In *Boletín bibliográfico de la Secretaría de Hacienda y Crédito Público* 232, no. 1. Mexico City: Secretaría de Hacienda y Crédito Público.

Castañeda, Antonia I. 1990. Presidiarias y Pobladoras: Spanish-Mexican Women in Frontier Monterey, Alta California, 1770–1821. Ph.D. diss., Stanford University.

Castañeda, Carmen. 1989. *Violación, estupro y sexualidad. Nueva Galicia. 1790–1821.* Mexico City: Editorial Hexágona.

Castellanos, Rosario. 1973. *Mujer que sabe latín.* Colección SEP/Setentas. Mexico City: SEP.

———. 1975. *El eterno femenino.* Colección Popular. Mexico City: Fondo de Cultura Económica.

Castillo, Pedro G., and Antonio Ríos Bustamante. 1989. *México en Los Angeles: Una historia social y cultural, 1781–1985.* Los Noventa. Mexico City: CONACULTA, Alianza Editorial Mexicana.

CEHSMO. 1975. *La mujer y el movimiento obrero mexicano en el siglo XIX. Antología de la Prensa Obrera.* Mexico City: Centro de Estudios Históricos del Movimiento Obrero Mexicano.

Chabaud, Jacqueline. 1975. *Educación y promoción de la mujer.* Colección SEP/Setentas 227. Mexico City: SEP.

Chávez Orozco, Luis. 1977. Diálogo diez y seis entre doña Clara Verdad y doña Juana Valiente. In *La agonía del artesanado.* Cuadernos Obreros 17. Mexico City: CEHSMO.

Chipman, Donald. 1981. "Isabel Moctezuma: Pioneer of *Mestizaje.*" In *Struggle and Survival in Colonial America,* ed. David Sweet and Gary Nash, pp. 214–227. Berkeley: University of California Press.

CONAPO. 1975a. *Los derechos de la mujer.* Mexico City: CONAPO, Secretaría de Gobernación. Documents.

———. 1975b. *La igualdad de la mujer.* Mexico City: CONAPO, Secretaría de Gobernación. Documents.

Conde, Teresa del. 1976. *Vida de Frida Kahlo.* Mexico City: Secretaría de la Presidencia.

Cortés Jácome, María Elena. 1982. "Negros amancebados con indias, siglo XVI." In *Familia y sexualidad en la Nueva España. Memoria del Primer Simposio de Historia de las Mentalidades: Familia, Matrimonio y Sexualidad en la Nueva España.* Colección SEP/Ochentas 41. Mexico City: Fondo de Cultura Económica-SEP.

Couturier, Edith. 1978. "Women in a Noble Family: The Mexican Counts of Regla, 1750–1830." In *Latin American Women: Historical Perspectives,* ed. Asunción Lavrin, pp. 129–149. Westport, Conn.: Greenwood Press.

Dallal, Alberto. 1987. *El 'dancing' mexicano.* Lecturas Mexicanas 70. Mexico City: SEP-Oasis.

de la Cruz, Sor Juana Inés. [1690] 1929. *Respuesta a Sor Filotea de la Cruz.* Mexico City: La Voz Nueva.

Delegación Benito Juárez. 1980. *Evocación de las mujeres ilustres: Carmen Serdán, Gabriela Mistral, la marquesa Calderón de la Barca, Rosario Castellanos, María Enriqueta Camarillo de Pereyra, Josefa Murillo.* Mexico City: Publicaciones Delegación Benito Juárez.

Delgado, Rafael. [1904] 1961. *Los parientes ricos.* Colección de Escritores Mexicanos 6. Mexico City: Editorial Porrúa.

———. [1890] 1970. *La calandria.* Colección Sepan Cuántos 154. México City: Editorial Porrúa.

Díaz del Castillo, Bernal. 1942. *Historia verdadera de la Conquista de la Nueva España.* 2 vols. Mexico City: Editorial Porrúa.

Dublán, Manuel, and José Manuel Lozano. 1878. *Legislación Mexicana.* Mexico City: Imprenta del Comercio.

Echeverría, Bolívar. 1994. "Malintzin, la lengua." In *La Malinche, sus padres y sus hijos,* ed. Margo Glantz. Mexico City: UNAM-FFyL.

El hogar: Cartas sobre la educación del bello sexo. 1872. Mexico City: Instituto Literario de Toluca.

Elmendorf, Mary L. 1973. *La mujer maya y el cambio.* Colección SEP/Setentas 85. Mexico City: SEP.

Elú de Leñero, María del Carmen. 1975. *El trabajo de la mujer en México: Alternativas para el cambio.* Mexico City: Instituto Mexicano de Estudios Sociales.

Feijóo, Benito Jerónimo. 1863. "Defensa de las mujeres." in *Obras escogidas,* vol. 56. Madrid: Imprenta de Rivadenegra.

Fernández, Justino. 1959. *Coatlicue: Estética del arte indígena antiguo.* Estudios de Arte y Estética 12. Mexico City: IIE-UNAM.

Fernández de Lizardi, José Joaquín. 1955. *Heroínas mexicanas: María Leona Vicario, Mariana Rodríguez Lazarín, María Fermina Rivera, Manuela Herrera y otras.* Biblioteca de Historiadores Mexicanos. Mexico City: Vargas Rea Impresor.

Flores, Ana María. 1961. "La mujer en la sociedad." In *La Vida Social,* Vol. 2 of *México: Cincuenta años de revolución.* Mexico City: Fondo de Cultura Económica.

Flores Magón, Ricardo. 1970. "A la mujer." In *La Revolución Mexicana,* compiled by Adolfo Sánchez Rebolledo. Colección 70, no. 74. Mexico City: Editorial Grijalbo.

Formoso de Obregón Santacilia, Adela. 1940. *La mujer mexicana y la organización social del país.* Colección Denegre 2048. Mexico City: Talleres Gráficos de la Nación.

Foppa, Alaíde. 1979. "El Congreso de Yucatán, 1916." *Fem: Publicación Feminista Trimestral* 3 (11): 55–59.

Franco, Jean. 1989. *Plotting Women: Gender and Representation in Mexico.* London: Verso.

———. 1995. "La Malinche: Del don al contrato social." *Debate Feminista* 2 (April): 251–270.

French, William E. 1992. "Prostitutes and Guardian Angels: Women, Work, and the Family in Porfirian Mexico." *Hispanic American Historical Review* 72 (4): 529–553.

Gage, Thomas. 1982. *Nuevo reconocimiento de Las Indias Occidentales.* Colección SEP/Ochentas 38. Mexico City: SEP–Fondo de Cultura Económica.

Galeana, Benita. 1940. *Benita: Autobiografía.* Mexico City: Imprenta Rústica Donceles.

Gallagher, Ann Miriam. 1978. "The Indian Nuns of Mexico City's *Monasterio of Corpus Christi,* 1724–1821." In *Latin American Women: Historical Perspectives,* ed. Asunción Lavrin, pp. 150–172. Westport, Conn.: Greenwood Press.

———. 1985. "Las monjas indígenas del monasterio de Corpus Christi de la Ciudad de Mexico City: 1724–1821." In *Las mujeres latinoamericanas,* ed. Asunción Lavrin. Colección Tierra Firme. Mexico City: Fondo de Cultura Económica.

García, Ana Lidia. 1994. *Problemas metodológicos de la historia de las mujeres: La historiografía dedicada al siglo XIX mexicano.* Mexico City: UNAM-PUEG.

García, Genaro. 1891. *Apuntes sobre la condición de la mujer.* Mexico City: Compañía Limitada de Tipografía.

———. 1910. *Leona Vicario: Heroína insurgente.* Mexico City: Museo Nacional de Arqueología, Historia y Etnología.

García Ayluardo, Clara, and Manuel Ramos Medina (coordinators). 1994. *Manifestaciones religiosas en el mundo colonial: Mujeres, instituciones y culto a María.* Centro de Estudios de Historia de México. Mexico City: Universidad Iberoamericana (Departamento de Historia)–INAH (DEH)-CONDUMEX.

García Flores, Margarita. 1979. *¿Sólo para mujeres?* Mexico City: Radio UNAM.

García Mundo, Octavio. 1976. *El movimiento inquilinario de Veracruz, 1922.* Colección SEP/Setentas 269. Mexico City: SEP.

García Somonte, Mariano. 1969. *Doña Marina, "La Malinche."* Mexico City: EDIMEX.

Garibay Kintana, Angel María. 1965. *Teogonía e historia de los mexicanos: Tres opúsculos del siglo XVI.* Colección Sepan Cuántos. Mexico City: Editorial Porrúa.

Garza Tarazona, Silvia. 1991. *La mujer mesoamericana.* Mexico City: Editorial Planeta.

Giraud, François. 1982. "De las problemáticas europeas al caso novohispano: Apuntes para una historia de la familia mexicana." In *Familia y sexualidad en la Nueva España,* DEH-INAH, pp. 56–80. *Memoria del Primer Simposio de Historia de las Mentalidades: Familia, Matrimonio y Sexualidad en la Nueva España.* Colección SEP/Ochentas 41. Mexico City: Fondo de Cultura Económica-SEP.

Glantz, Margo. 1995. *Sor Juana Inés de la Cruz: ¿Hagiografía o autobiografía?* Mexico City: Grijalbo-UNAM.

Gómez de Orozco, Federico. 1942. *Doña Marina: La dama de la conquista.* Mexico City: Editorial Xóchitl.

Gomezjara, Francisco, Estanislao Barrera, and Nicolás Pérez. 1978. *Sociología de la prostitución.* Mexico City: Editorial Nueva Sociología.

Gonzalbo Aizpuru, Pilar, ed. 1985. *La educación de la mujer en la Nueva España.* Mexico City: SEP-El Caballito.

————. 1987a. *Las mujeres en la Nueva España. Educación y vida cotidiana.* Mexico City: El Colegio de México.

————. 1987b. "Tradición y ruptura en la educación femenina del siglo XVI." In *Presencia y transparencia: La mujer en la historia de México,* ed. Carmen Ramos Escandón. Mexico City: El Colegio de México.

Gonzalbo Aizpuru, Pilar, and Cecilia Rabell, comps. 1994. *La familia en el mundo iberoamericano.* Mexico City: UNAM-IIS.

González Montes, Soledad, and Pilar Iracheta. 1987. "La violencia en la vida de las mujeres campesinas: El distrito de Tenango, 1880–1910." In *Presencia y transparencia: La mujer en la historia de México,* ed. Carmen Ramos Escandón. Mexico City: El Colegio de México.

Gooch, Fanny Chambers. 1887. *Face to Face with the Mexicans.* New York: Fords, Howard and Hulbert.

Gruzinski, Serge. 1979. "Historia de la sexualidad: Metodología." In *Introducción a la historia de las mentalidades.* Seminario de Historia de las Mentalidades y la Religión en México. Cuaderno de Trabajo 24. Mexico City: DEH-INAH.

————. 1985. "Las cenizas del deseo: Homosexuales novohispanos a mediados del siglo XVII." In *De la santidad a la perversión, o de por qué no se cumplía la ley de Dios en la sociedad novohispana,* ed. Sergio Ortega. Mexico City: Enlace-Grijalbo.

Guerrero, Julio. 1901. *La génesis del crimen en México: Estudio de psiquiatría social.* Paris: Librairie de Ch. Bouret.

Gutiérrez, Ramón A. 1991. *When Jesus Came, the Corn Mothers Went Away: Marriage, Sexuality, and Power in New Mexico, 1500–1846.* Stanford: Stanford University Press.

Hellbom, Anna Britta. 1967. *La participación cultural de las mujeres indias y mestizas en el México precortesiano y postrevolucionario.* Monograph Series 10. Stockholm: Etnografische Museet.

Hernández, Ana María. 1940. *La mujer mexicana en la industria textil.* Mexico City: Tipografía Moderna.

Herrera, Hayden. 1983. *Frida: Una biografía de Frida Kahlo.* Mexico City: Editorial Diana.

Hidalgo, Berta. 1980. *El movimiento femenino en México.* Mexico City: EDAMEX.

Hierro, Graciela. 1989. *De la domesticación a la educación de las mexicanas.* Mexico City: Editorial Torres Asociados.

INAH. 1985. *La mujer en la resistencia contra el invasor.* Mexico City: Museo Nacional de las Intervenciones. Pamphlet.

Inclán, Luis G. [1869] 1969. *Astucia: El jefe de los hermanos de la hoja o los charros contrabandistas de la Rama.* Colección Sepan Cuántos 63. Mexico City: Editorial Porrúa.

INEGI. 1995. *La mujer mexicana: Un balance estadístico al final del siglo XX.* Mexico City: INEGI-UNIFEM (Fondo de Desarrollo de Naciones Unidas para la Mujer).

INEHRM, Honorable Cámara de Diputados, LV Legislatura. 1992. *Las mujeres en la Revolución mexicana: Biografías de mujeres revolucionarias, 1884–1920.* Mexico City: INEHRM–Secretaría de Gobernación.

INFONAVIT. 1975. *1916: Primer Congreso Feminista de México.* Mexico City: INFONAVIT.

Katz, Joseph, ed. 1970. *Stephen Crane in the West and Mexico.* Kent, Ohio: Kent University Press.

Keremitsis, Dawn. 1973. *La industria textil en el siglo XIX.* Colección SEP/ Setentas 67. Mexico City: SEP.

Kolonitz, Paula. 1984. *Un viaje a México en 1864.* Colección Lecturas Mexicanas 41. Mexico City: SEP–Fondo de Cultura Económica.

Lara y Pardo, Luis. 1908. *La prostitución en México.* Mexico City: Librería de Ch. Bouret.

Lau, Ana. 1987. *La nueva ola del feminismo.* Mujeres en Su Tiempo. Mexico City: Planeta.

Lau, Ana, and Carmen Ramos. 1993. *Mujeres y Revolución, 1900–1917.* Mexico City: INEHRM-INAH.

Lavrin, Asunción. 1965. "Ecclesiastical Reform of Nunneries in New Spain in the Eighteenth Century." *The Americas* 22, no. 2 (October): 182–203.

———. 1971. "Problems and Policies in the Administration of Nunneries in Mexico, 1785–1835." *The Americas* 28(1) (July): 57–77.

———. 1976. "Women in Convents, Their Economic and Social Role in Colonial Mexico." In *Liberating Women's History,* ed. Berenice Carroll. London: Greenwood Press.

———. 1981. "Las mujeres tienen la palabra: Otras voces en la historia de México." *Historia Mexicana* (El Colegio de México) 31 (2): 278–313.

———. 1984. "Aproximación histórica en el tema de la sexualidad en el México colonial." *Encuentro* (Guadalajara: El Colegio de Jalisco) 2, no. 1 (October– December): 23–39.

———. 1985. "Investigación sobre la mujer de la colonia en México: Siglos XVII y XVIII." In *Las mujeres latinoamericanas: Perspectivas históricas,* ed. Asunción Lavrin. Colección Tierra Firma. Mexico City: Fondo de Cultura Económica.

Lavrin, Asunción, ed. 1978. *Latin American Women: Historical Perspectives.* Contributions in Women's Studies, no. 3. Westport, Conn.: Greenwood Press.

———, ed. 1991. *Sexualidad y matrimonio en la América Hispánica.* Mexico City: CONACULTA-Grijalbo.

León, Fray Luis de. 1946. *La perfecta casada.* Colección Austral 51. Buenos Aires and Mexico City: Espasa-Calpe Argentina.

León Portilla, Miguel. 1972. *Visión de los vencidos: Relaciones indígenas de la conquista.* Biblioteca del Estudiante Universitario 81. Mexico City: UNAM.

———. 1974. *La filosofía náhuatl estudiada en sus fuentes.* Serie Monografías de Cultura Náhuatl 10. Mexico City: IIH-UNAM.

———. 1975. *La familia náhuatl prehispánica.* Mexico City: INPI.

Ley de Matrimonio Civil (July 23, 1859). In *Documentos constitucionales y legales relativos a la función judicial, 1810–1917,* 3 vols., ed. Lucio Cabrera Acevedo, vol. 2, pp. 223–226. Mexico City: Suprema Corte de Justicia de la Nación, 1997.

López Austin, Alfredo. 1980. *Cuerpo humano e ideología: Los conceptos de los antiguos nahuas.* Serie Antropológica 39, 2 vols. Mexico City: UNAM.

———. 1982. "La sexualidad entre los antiguos nahuas." In *Familia y sexualidad en Nueva España. Memoria del Primer Simposio de Historia de las Mentalidades: Familia, matrimonio y sexualidad en Nueva España.* Colección Sep/Ochentas 41. Mexico City: Fondo de Cultura Económica–SEP.

———. 1991. "La sexualidad entre los antiguos nahuas." In *Época prehispánica*, vol. 1 of *El Álbum de la mujer: Antología ilustrada de las mexicanas*, ed. Enriqueta Tuñón Pablos. Colección Divulgación. Mexico City: INAH.

Macías, Anna. 1978. "Felipe Carrillo Puerto and Women's Liberation in Mexico." In *Latin American Women: Historical Perspectives*, ed. Asunción Lavrin, pp. 286–301. Westport, Conn.: Greenwood Press.

———. 1980. "Women and the Mexican Revolution." *The Americas* 37, no. 1 (July): 53–82.

———. 1982. *Against All Odds: The Feminist Movement in Mexico to 1940.* Westpoint, Conn.: Greenwood Press.

Malvido, Adriana. 1995. *Nahui Ollin: La mujer del sol.* Mexico City: Diana.

Malvido, Elsa. 1990. "El uso del cuerpo femenino en la época colonial mexicana a través de los estudios de demografía histórica." In *Between Borders: Essays on Mexicana/Chicana History*, ed. Adelaida R. del Castillo. La Mujer Latina Series. Encino, Calif.: Floricanto Press.

Maza, Francisco de la. 1981. *El guadalupanismo mexicano.* Mexico City: Fondo de Cultura Económica.

Mendieta Alatorre, María de los Ángeles. 1961. *La mujer en la Revolución mexicana.* Biblioteca del Instituto Nacional de Estudios Históricos de la Revolución Mexicana 23. Mexico City: Talleres Gráficos de la Nación.

———. 1972. *Margarita Maza de Juárez.* Mexico City: Comisión para la Conmemoración del Fallecimiento de Benito Juárez.

Molina Enríquez, Andrés. [1905] 1972. "El problema político." In *Positivismo y porfirismo*, ed. Abelardo Villegas. Colección SEP/Setentas 40. Mexico City: SEP.

Monjarás-Ruiz, Jesús, ed. 1975. *Los primeros días de la Revolución: Testimonios periodísticos alemanes.* Colección SEP/Setentas 220. Mexico City: SEP.

Monsiváis, Carlos. 1979. "Sexismo en la literatura mexicana." In *Imagen y realidad de la mujer*, ed. Elena Urrutia. Colección SEP/Setentas-Diana 172. Mexico City: SEP.

———. 1993. "El día de la primera votación." *La Jornada*, October 21, p. 1.

Moreno Toscano, Alejandra. 1981. "El siglo de la Conquista." In Vol. 1 of *Historia general de México.* 2 vols. Mexico City: El Colegio de México.

Mörner, Magnus. 1974. *Estado, razas y cambio social en la Hispanoamérica colonial.* Colección SEP/Setentas 128. Mexico City: SEP.

Muriel, Josefina. 1946. *Conventos de monjas en la Nueva España.* Mexico City: Editorial Santiago.

———. 1963. *Las indias caciques de Corpus Christi.* Serie Histórica 6. Mexico City: UNAM–Instituto de Historia.

———. 1974. *Los recogimientos de mujeres: Respuesta a una problemática social novohispana.* Serie Historia Novohispana 24. Mexico City: UNAM-IIH.

———. 1978. *Monjas coronadas.* Mexico City: Secretaría Particular de la Presidencia.

———. 1982. *Cultura femenina novohispana.* Serie Historia Novohispana 30. Mexico City: UNAM-IIH.

———. 1992. "Historia de la mujer en México." In *El historiador frente a la historia.* Mexico City: UNAM-IIH. Serie Divulgación 1.

Navarrete, Ifigenia Martínez de. 1969. *La mujer y los derechos sociales.* Mexico City: Editorial Oasis.

Núñez, Fernanda. 1995. "Malintzin." *Debate Feminista* (Mexico) 5, no. 3 (March): 51–59.

———. 1996. El juez, la prostituta y sus clientes: Discursos y representaciones sobre las prostitutas y la prostitución en la ciudad de México, en la segunda mitad del siglo XIX. Master's thesis, Escuela Nacional de Antropología e Historia.

Núñez y Domínguez, José de Jesús. 1950. *La virreina mexicana doña María Francisca de la Gándara de Calleja.* Mexico City: Imprenta Universitaria.

Ojeda, María de los Ángeles, and Cecilia Rossell. 1995. *Diosas y mujeres en códices prehispánicos: Borgia (Nahua-Mixteco) y Selden (Mixteco).* Mexico City: INAH.

Ortega, Juan. 1953. "Estudio preliminar a Brantz Mayer." In *México, lo que fue y lo que es,* ed. Juan Ortega. Colección Biblioteca Americana, Serie Viajeros. Mexico City: Fondo de Cultura Económica.

Ortega, Sergio, ed. 1985. *De la santidad a la perversión, o de por qué no se cumplía la ley de Dios en la sociedad novohispana.* Mexico City: Enlace-Grijalbo.

Ortega Martínez, Ana María. 1945. *Mujeres españolas en la conquista de México.* Mexico City: Vargas Rea Impresor.

Ortiz, Rina. 1975. "Josefina García viuda de García." *Historia Obrera* 2, no. 5 (June): 13–18.

Ots Capdequi, José María. 1976. *El estado español en Indias.* Mexico City: Fondo de Cultura Económica.

Parcero, María de la Luz. 1992. *Condición de la mujer en México durante el siglo XIX.* Colección Científica. Mexico City: INAH.

Payno, Manuel. [1843–1848] 1984. *Sobre mujeres, amores y matrimonios.* La Matraca, 2d ser., no. 3. Mexico City: Premiá Editores.

Paz, Octavio. 1982. *Sor Juana Inés de la Cruz, o Las trampas de la fe.* Biblioteca Breve. Spain: Seix Barral.

———. 1985. *The Labyrinth of Solitude.* Translated from the Spanish by Lysander Kemp, Yara Milos, and Rachel Phillips Belash. New York: Grove Press.

Piho, Virve. 1982. *La obrera textil: Encuesta sobre su trabajo, ingreso y vida familiar.* Serie La Industria 4. Mexico City: Centro de Estudios del Desarrollo, Facultad de Ciencias Políticas y Sociales, UNAM, Acta Sociológica.

Poniatowska, Elena. 1984. *Hasta no verte Jesús mío.* Mexico City: Era.

PRI. 1953. *Heroínas de México: Homenaje a la mujer mexicana.* Mexico City: PRI, Turanzas del Valle.

Quezada, Noemí. 1975. *Amor y magia amorosa entre los aztecas: Supervivencia en el México colonial.* Serie Antropológica 17. Mexico City: IIA.

———. 1994. "Amor, erotismo y deseo entre los mexicas y en el mundo colonial." *Antropológicas* 10 (April): 14–22.

Radkau, Verena. 1984. *"La Fama" y la vida: Una fábrica y sus obreras.* Cuadernos de la Casa Chata 108. Mexico City: CIESAS.

———. 1989. *Por la debilidad de nuestro ser; mujeres del "pueblo" en la paz porfiriana.* Cuadernos de la Casa Chata 108. Mexico City: CIESAS.

Ramírez, Ignacio. 1960. Vol. 2 of *Obras Completas.* Mexico City: Editora Nacional.

Ramírez, Santiago. 1983. *El mexicano: Psicología de sus motivaciones.* Mexico City: Editorial Grijalbo.

Ramírez Garrido, José Domingo. 1918. *Al margen del feminismo.* Colección de Escritos de Ramírez Garrido 8. Mérida, Yuc.: Talleres Pluma y Lápiz.

Ramos Escandón, Carmen, ed. 1987. *Presencia y transparencia: La mujer en la historia de México.* Mexico City: El Colegio de México.

Ramos Soriano, José Abel. 1982. "Lectores de libros prohibidos, Siglo XVIII." In *Familia y sexualidad en Nueva España. Memoria del Primer Simposio de Historia de las Mentalidades: Familia, matrimonio y sexualidad en Nueva España.* Historia de las Mentalidades. Colección SEP/Ochentas 41. Mexico City: Fondo de Cultura Económica–SEP.

Rascón, María Antonieta. 1979. "La mujer y la lucha social." In *Imagen y realidad de la mujer,* ed. Elena Urrutia. Colección SEP/Setentas-Diana 172. Mexico City: SEP.

Recopilación de Leyes de los Reynos de las Indias [1681] 1973. Prologue by Ramón Menéndez Pidal. 4 vols. Madrid: Ediciones Cultura Hispánica. (Edición facsimilar de la edición de Julián de Paredes, 1681.)

Reed, John. 1969. *Insurgent Mexico.* A Clarion Book. New York: Simon and Schuster. Published in Spanish as *México insurgente* (Barcelona: Ariel, 1969).

Regueiro, María del Carmen, Norma Márquez, and Atanasio Gutiérrez. 1981. *La mujer en sus actividades.* Colección de Fotografías de Lázaro Blanco. Mexico City: SPP.

Reyes, Aurelio de los. 1973. *Los orígenes del cine en México (1896–1900).* Cuadernos de Cine, no. 21. Mexico City: UNAM (Dirección General de Difusión Cultural).

———. 1992. *Con Villa en México: Testimonios de camarógrafos norteamericanos, 1911–1916.* Mexico City: UNAM (IIE)–Dirección General de Actividades Cinematográficas–Secretaría de Gobernación: INEHRM.

Reyes, Aurelio de los, ed. 1981. *Cine y sociedad en México, 1896–1930.* Vol. 1, *Vivir de sueños (1896–1920).* Mexico City: UNAM-IIE. Cineteca Nacional.

———, ed. 1993. *Cine y sociedad en México, 1896–1930.* Vol. 2, *Bajo el cielo de México (1920–1924).* Mexico City: UNAM-IIE.

Robles Cahero, José Antonio. 1985. "La memoria del cuerpo y la transmisión cultural: Las danzas populares en el siglo XVIII." *La memoria y el olvido.* Segundo Simposio de Historia de las Mentalidades. Colección Científica 144. Mexico City: INAH-SEP.

Robles de Mendoza, Margarita. 1931. *La evolución de la mujer mexicana.* Mexico City: Imprenta Galas.

Rocha, Marta Eva, ed. 1991. *El porfiriato y la Revolución,* vol. 4 of *El Álbum de la mujer: Antología ilustrada de las mexicanas.* Colección Divulgación. Mexico City: INAH.

Rodríguez, María de Jesús. 1987. "La mujer y la familia en la sociedad mexica." In *Presencia y transparencia: La mujer en la historia de México,* ed. Carmen Ramos Escandón. Mexico City: El Colegio de México.

———. 1988. *La mujer azteca.* Mexico City: Editorial Universidad Autónoma del Estado de México.

Rodríguez Cabo, Mathilde. 1937. *La mujer y la Revolución.* Colección Denegre 1388. Mexico City: Frente Socialista de Abogados.

Romero, Emilia. 1948. *Mujeres de América*. Biblioteca Enciclopédica Popular 196. Mexico City: SEP.

Romero, José Rubén. 1991. "La familia indígena noble y la conservación de un poder disminuido." In *Familia y poder en Nueva España. Memoria del Tercer Simposio de Historia de las Mentalidades*. Colección Científica 228. Mexico City: INAH.

Romero de Terreros, Manuel. 1944. *Bocetos de la vida social en la Nueva España*. Mexico City: Editorial Posada.

Romo, Marta. 1979. "¿Y las soldaderas? Tomasa García toma la palabra." *Fem: Publicación Feminista Trimestral* 3: 11 (Nov.–Dec.): 12–14.

Ros, María Amparo. 1985. "La real fábrica de tabaco: ¿Un embrión del capitalismo?" *Historias* 10 (July–September): 51–63.

Rubio Siliceo, Luis. 1929. *Mujeres célebres en la independencia de México*. Mexico City: Talleres Gráficos de la Nación.

Ruiz Gaytán, Beatriz. 1979. "Un grupo trabajador importante no incluido en la historia laboral mexicana: Trabajadoras domésticas." In *El trabajo y los trabajadores en la historia de México/The Labor and Laborers through Mexican History*, ed. Elsa Cecilia Frost, Michael C. Meyer, Josefina Zoraida Vázquez, with the collaboration of Lilia Díaz. Mexico City: El Colegio de México–University of Arizona Press.

Sáenz Royo, Artemisa. 1954. *Historia político-social-cultural del movimiento femenino en México, 1914–1950*. Mexico City: Editorial M. León Sánchez.

Sagredo, Rafael. 1996. *María Villa (a) La chiquita. num. 4002. Un parásito social del porfiriato*. Los Libros de la Condesa. Mexico City: Editorial Cal y Arena.

Sahagún, Bernardino de. 1956. *Historia general de las cosas de Nueva España*. 4 vols. Mexico City: Editorial Porrúa.

Salas, Elizabeth. 1995. *Soldaderas en los ejércitos mexicanos: Mitos e historia*. Mexico City: Diana.

Salazar, Flora. 1987. Los sirvientes domésticos y sus amos en la ciudad de México en el siglo XIX. Master's thesis, Escuela Nacional de Antropología e Historia.

Schneider, Luis Mario. 1987. *Obras completas de María Antonieta Rivas Mercado*. Mexico City: Editorial Oasis.

Seed, Patricia. 1988. *To Love, Honor, and Obey in Colonial Mexico: Conflicts over Marriage Choice, 1574–1821*. Stanford: Stanford University Press.

———. 1994. "La narrativa de Don Juan: El lenguaje de la seducción en la literatura y la sociedad hispánica del Siglo XVII." In *La familia en el mundo iberoamericano*, compiled by Pilar Gonzalbo and Cecilia Rabell, pp. 91–125. Mexico City: UNAM–IIS.

Seminario de Historia de las Mentalidades. 1979. *Introducción a la historia de las mentalidades*. Cuaderno de Trabajo 24. Mexico City: DEH–INAH.

———. 1980. *Seis ensayos sobre el discurso colonial relativo a la comunidad doméstica*. Cuaderno de Trabajo 35. Mexico City: DEH–INAH.

———. 1982. *Familia y sexualidad en la Nueva España. Memoria del Primer Simposio de Historia de las Mentalidades: Familia, matrimonio y sexualidad en la Nueva España*. Colección SEP/Ochentas 41. Mexico City: Fondo de Cultura Económica–SEP.

———. 1985. *La memoria y el olvido. Segundo Simposio de Historia de las Mentalidades*. Colección Científica 144. Mexico City: INAH–SEP.

―――. 1987. *El placer de pecar y el afán de normar*. Contrapuntos. Mexico City: Joaquín Mortíz.

―――. 1989. *Del dicho al hecho . . . Transgresiones y pautas culturales en la Nueva España*. Colección Científica. Mexico City: INAH.

―――. 1991. *Familia y poder en Nueva España. Memoria del Tercer Simposio de Historia de las Mentalidades*. Colección Científica. Mexico City: INAH.

Sheridan, Cecilia. 1983. *Mujer obrera y organización sindical: El sindicato de obreras desmanchadoras de café, Coatepec, Veracruz: Un estudio histórico-monográfico*. Cuadernos de la Casa Chata. Mexico City: CIESAS.

Soto, Shirlene Ann. 1990. *Emergence of the Modern Mexican Woman: Her Participation in Revolution and Struggle for Equality, 1910–1940*. Women and Modern Revolution Series. Denver: Arden Press.

Stern, Steve J. 1995. *The Secret History of Gender, Women, Men, and Power in Late Colonial Mexico*. Chapel Hill: University of North Carolina Press.

Suárez, Marcela, and Guadalupe Ríos. 1992. "Las prostitutas y el estado en la época porfiriana." *Fem: Publicación Feminista Trimestral* 16, no. 111 (May): 4–9.

Sweeny, Judith. 1981. "Chicana History: A Review of the Literature." In *Essays on la Mujer*, ed. Rosana Sánchez and Rosa Martínez Cruz. Los Angeles: Chicano Studies Center Publications, UCLA.

Sweet, David, and Gary Nash, eds. 1981. *Struggle and Survival in Colonial America*. Berkeley: University of California Press.

Tibol, Raquel. 1977. *Frida Kahlo: Crónica, testimonios y aproximaciones*. Mexico City: Ediciones de Cultura Popular.

Todorov, Tzvetan. 1982. *La conquête de l'Amerique: La question de l'autre*. Paris: Seuil. In Spanish: *La conquista de América: La cuestión del otro*. Mexico City: Siglo Veintiuno Editores, 1987.

Tostado Gutiérrez, Marcela, ed. 1991. *Época colonial*, vol. 2 of *El Albúm de la mujer: Antología ilustrada de las mexicanas*. Colección Divulgación. Mexico City: INAH.

Tuñón Pablos, Enriqueta. 1987. "La lucha política de la mujer mexicana por el derecho al sufragio y sus repercusiones." In *Presencia y transparencia: La mujer en la historia de México*, ed. Carmen Ramos Escandón. Mexico City: El Colegio de México.

Tuñón Pablos, Enriqueta, ed. 1991. *Época prehispánica*, vol. 1 of *El Albúm de la mujer: Antología ilustrada de las mexicanas*. Colección Divulgación. Mexico City: INAH.

Tuñón, Esperanza. 1992. *Mujeres que se organizan: El Frente Único pro-Derechos de la Mujer, 1935–1938*. Mexico City: UNAM–Miguel Ángel Porrúa.

―――. 1997. *Mujeres en escena: De la tramoya al protagonismo. El quehacer político del movimiento amplio de mujeres en México (1982–1994)*. Mexico City: UNAM–El Colegio de la Frontera Sur–Miguel Ángel Porrúa.

Tuñón, Julia, ed. 1991. *El siglo XIX (1821–1880)*, vol. 3 of *El Albúm de la mujer: Antología ilustrada de las mexicanas*. Colección Divulgación. Mexico City: INAH.

Turner, Frederick. 1967. "Los efectos de la participación femenina en la Revolución de 1910." *Historia Mexicana* 16, no. 4 (April–June): 603–620.

Tutino, John Mark. 1983. "Power, Class, and Family: Men and Women in the Mexican Elite, 1750–1810." *The Americas* 39, no. 2 (January): 359–381.

———. 1985. "Guerra, comercio colonial y textiles mexicanos: El Bajío, 1585–1810." *Historias*, no. 11 (October–December): 35–45.

Urrutia, Elena, ed. 1979. *Imagen y realidad de la mujer.* Colección SEP/Setentas-Diana. Mexico City: SEP.

Valdés Echenique, Teresa, and Enrique Gomariz Moraga, coords. 1995. *Mujeres latinoamericanas en cifras: México.* Santiago, Chile: Instituto de la Mujer (Ministerio de Asuntos Sociales)–FLACSO (Facultad Latinoamericana de Ciencias Sociales).

Vidales, Susana. 1980. "Ni madres abnegadas, ni adelitas." *Críticas de la economía política: Edición latinoamericana. La mujer: Trabajo y política,* no. 14–15 (April–June): 241–281.

Viveros Pabello, Guadalupe. 1993. *Mi padre revolucionario.* Colección Testimonios. Mexico City: INEHRM–Secretaría de Gobernación.

Vives, Juan Luis. 1940. *Instrucción de la mujer cristiana.* Colección Austral 138. Mexico City–Buenos Aires: Espasa-Calpe Argentina.

Wollstonecraft, Mary. 1977. *Vindicación de los derechos de la mujer.* Madrid: Editorial Debate.

Woolf, Virginia. [1929] 1957. *A Room of One's Own.* New York and London: Harcourt Brace Jovanovich.

Zamora, Marta. 1987. *Frida: El pincel de la angustia.* Mexico City: N.p.

Zarco, Francisco. [1850–1851] 1968. *Escritos literarios.* Mexico City: Editorial Porrúa. Colección Sepan Cuántos 90.

Journals That Devote Special Issues to the Topic

Boletín del Archivo General de la Nación, 3d ser., 3, no. 9 (July–September 1979).

Encuentro. Estudios sobre la mujer 2, no. 5 (October–December 1984). Guadalajara: El Colegio de Jalisco.

Fem: Publicación Feminista Trimestral 3, no. 11 (November–December 1979). Mexico City: Nueva Cultura Feminista.

Historia Obrera 2, no. 5 (June 1975). Mexico City: CEHSMO.

Nueva Antropología: Revista de Ciencias Sociales. "Estudios sobre la mujer: Problemas teóricos." 8, no. 30 (November 1986).

Bibliographies

Arbeláez A., María Soledad, Concepción Ruiz Funes, Marcela Tostado Guriérrez, Enriqueta Tuñón Pablos, and Julia Tuñón Pablos. 1983. *Bibliografía comentada sobre la mujer mexicana.* Cuaderno de Trabajo 55. Mexico City: DEH-INAH.

Bartra, Eli, Elia Ramírez, Nina Torres, Angeles Sánchez. 1983. *Mujer: Una bibliografía. México.* Mexico City: UAM-Xochimilco.

Bibliografía de cursos, seminarios y talleres del Programa Interdisciplinario de Estudios de la Mujer. 1996. Mexico City: El Colegio de México.

Índice de la revista FEM (1964–1989). 1990. Mexico City: DEMAC (Documentación y Estudios de Mujeres, Asociación Civil).

Parcero, María de la Luz. 1982. *La mujer en el siglo XIX en México: Bibliografía.* Mexico City: INAH.

Index

CPSIA information can be obtained at www.ICGtesting.com
Printed in the USA
BVOW07s0720060114

340913BV00001B/14/P